EVANGELICAL HOLINESS
AND OTHER ADDRESSES

By the same author:

Archibald G. Brown: Spurgeon's Successor
Heroes
Lloyd-Jones: Messenger of Grace
Pentecost—Today? The Biblical Basis for Understanding Revival
The Life of Martyn Lloyd-Jones (1899–1981)
The Old Evangelicalism: Old Truths for a New Awakening

EVANGELICAL HOLINESS
AND OTHER ADDRESSES

Iain H. Murray

THE BANNER OF TRUTH TRUST

THE BANNER OF TRUTH TRUST

3 Murrayfield Road, Edinburgh EH12 6EL, UK
P.O. Box 621, Carlisle, PA 17013, USA

*

© Iain H. Murray 2013

ISBN

Print: 978-1-84871-319-2
EPUB: 978-1-84871-320-8
Kindle: 978-1-84871-321-5

*

Typeset in 11/14 pt Minion Pro at
The Banner of Truth Trust, Edinburgh
Printed in the USA by
Versa Press, Inc.,
East Peoria, IL

CONTENTS

EVANGELICAL HOLINESS AND SPIRITUALITY[1]

This Keswick Convention has now existed for 135 years, and if it be asked whether there has been any one great theme that has run through these years, the answer is that there has: it has been the need for holiness in the life of the Christian. Why has there been such a concentration of attention on one subject? I believe it can be explained by answering another question: What is the means that God commonly uses to show the truth of the gospel message? It is surely the evidence of changed lives. There is an argument which the world cannot answer—when the selfish become caring, the proud humble, the immoral pure. It is spiritual men and women that make the gospel visible in the world. Christians are people very different from what they were, and very different from the society in which they live. They shine as lights 'in the midst of a crooked and perverse nation' (*Phil.* 2:15). Authentic holiness draws attention to God: 'Let your light so shine before men, that they may see your good works, and glorify your Father which is in heaven' (*Matt.* 5:16).

We live at a time and in a country where there is massive indifference to Christianity. Unbelief is arrogant. In many parts

[1] A lecture at the Keswick Convention, July 28, 2010.

of the land church buildings are disused and sold, perhaps to be turned into theatres or public houses. It might therefore be argued that the priorities for Christians today should be reaching the world outside, or defending the truth of the Christian faith. Both are certainly necessary, but the old Keswick priority remains the right one. When Christianity is weak, the fault generally lies not in the world but in the church herself. Let the spiritual health of the church be what it ought to be and there will be no question of her declining impact on the world. 'Study to show yourself approved unto God', is the biblical mandate; it is sanctified men and women who are described as being 'useful to the Master, prepared for every good work' (2 *Tim.* 2:15, 21). Speaking on this point, an old writer has said: 'The design of Christianity is to change men's lives. And if it does not prove its divinity by its efficacy, let it be condemned as an imposture. This was one of its most operative convincing proofs at the beginning, and certainly is its greatest abiding proof.'[1]

Take one of endless examples. There was in Kilmarnock, Scotland, a medical doctor named Robert Kalley. His upbringing had been one of nominal Christianity, before his studies at the University of Glasgow led him first to question the reliability of the Bible and then to become an open unbeliever. Once settled in his medical practice he gave his leisure hours to socialising, and soon gained the nickname, 'The dancing doctor of Kilmarnock'. Among his patients were Christians, one of them was a woman dying from cancer. Others of his patients were also Christians, and he pitied them for their lack of education. But on his visits

[1] Thomas Adam, *Private Thoughts on Religion* (London: Religious Tract Society, n.d.), p. 44.

to this woman he saw something which he could not explain; he would find her possessed of a peace stronger than her painful condition. She did not miss seeing his surprise and, pointing to what lay beside her bed, told him, 'Read the Book! It's all in the Book!' That witness led Kalley to become a new man and, in due course, a pioneer missionary in Madeira and Brazil.[1]

While holiness is a subject of permanent importance, it is also of particular relevance at the present time. You must have noticed how the word 'spirituality' has become fashionable. About a year ago I heard a member of the government speaking of the need for more money to be allocated for the promotion of 'spirituality'. I am told that in primary schools today 'spirituality' is a subject on the curriculum. If you visit many secular bookshops and ask what they have on 'spirituality' they will have no problem in directing you to some of their shelves.

Last month—June 2010—the Chancellor of Lincoln Cathedral complained that many people were describing themselves as 'spiritual but not religious'. Was his complaint in order? Should we not be glad people are recognizing that it is not enough to live for material things, and that we have a 'spirit' as well as a body? Don't we want the government to promote spirituality?

These questions cannot be answered without clarifying the meaning of words, for what we have here is a confusion of meaning. By 'spirituality' the government minister I heard explained that he meant such things as music, the arts, and the aesthetic. 'Music unlocks the key to their souls', it is said with regard to children. Others use the term 'spirituality' to describe finding

[1] I have written of him in the chapter 'Two Men and an Island' in *Heroes* (Edinburgh; The Banner of Truth Trust, 2009).

self-fulfilment in mysticism, in ascetic disciplines, or in transcendental meditation. Even prayer may be linked to spirituality, provided it is directed to the god of the individual's choice. So when we talk about evangelical holiness, and what it means to be spiritual, it is necessary to show that the words mean something very different to the current popular understanding of 'spirituality'.

There are two words commonly used for our subject in the Greek New Testament. One (*hagios*) is the basis for our words rendered 'holiness' or 'sanctification'; the other (*eusebeia*) is translated 'godliness'. Nine times, for instance, 'godliness' occurs in the pastoral epistles. Titus is to defend the truth which is 'according to godliness'; Timothy is told to exercise himself 'unto godliness'. It is perhaps strange that our leading modern versions retain the King James word 'godliness' in translating the original when, regrettably, 'godliness' is a word which is falling out of use. But it gets at the heart of what the New Testament means about holiness in the Christian. Holiness is the image of God visibly expressed. Holiness is God-likeness. Certainly Christianity produces morality—it changes the behaviour of men and women towards one another—but that does not come first. Holiness has first reference to what a person is before God; it speaks of love for God, reverence for God, glorifying God. Thus the churches of Judea, Galilee and Samaria are described as 'walking in the fear of the Lord, and in the comfort of the Holy Spirit' (*Acts* 9:31). Paul describes the Christians at Thessalonica as people who had 'turned to God from idols to serve the living and true God; and to wait for his Son from heaven' (*1 Thess.* 1:9, 10).

Three distinguishing evangelical truths

1. No man or woman is born in a state of holiness. There are no seeds of godliness within us that simply need to be nurtured and cultivated. All mankind fell in Adam and became strangers to God. The Bible draws a sharp line between what we were as originally created, and what we have become as sinners. Our likeness to God has gone. 'God is light and in him is no darkness at all (*1 John* 1:5). But we are in darkness, and love the darkness. 'There is none righteous, not even one; there is none who understands, there is none that seeks for God' (*Rom.* 3:10, 11) Other words by which the New Testament often states the difference between what we are in sin, and what we need to be, are the words 'the flesh' and 'spiritual'. No one is spiritual until they have the Holy Spirit, and no one has the Spirit until they are born again by the Spirit of God. 'That which is born of the flesh is flesh, and that which is born of the Spirit is spirit. Do not be amazed that I said unto you, "You must be born again"' (*John* 3:6, 7). ('Flesh' here does not mean 'body', it means fallen human nature. A Christian is still in the body, but he is not in 'the flesh'.)

There was a poll taken in the United States in recent times which showed that, of people surveyed, seventy-four per cent did not believe in orginal sin. The poll was a waste of time because by nature one hundred per cent of people do not actually believe in original sin. That is why true spiritual experience has to begin with God convicting us of sin. We do not believe we are born with sinful hearts, at enmity to God. We think sin is something people may or may not choose to do as they grow up. But the Bible teaches that we are all born alienated from God, 'dead in trespasses and sins', and 'by nature the children of wrath' (*Eph.* 2:3).

5

This was the teaching of Christ that so offended the Jewish religious leaders. They saw no need of a second birth because they saw nothing wrong with their first birth. They were blind to the truth that we 'go astray from the womb'—born with hearts described by God as 'desperately wicked' (*Jer.* 17:9). 'Out of the heart proceed evil thoughts, murders, adulteries, fornications, thefts, false witness, blasphemies' (*Matt.* 15:19).

Go to the pages of modern books on spirituality and you will find no such teaching. They teach that man is good at heart and only in need of improvement and uplift. Evangelicals have always been in collision with such teaching. The Methodist preachers of the eighteenth century were instructed to 'frequently insist on the doctrine of original sin. It is not stale or worn out; it is fundamental.'[1]

2. Evangelical holiness always follows submission to the Bible as the word of God. The church at Thessalonica was marked by the holiness of its members, and that happened, Paul reminds them, 'because when you received the word of God which you heard of us, you received it not as the word of men, but as it is in truth, the word of God, which effectually works also in you that believe' (*1 Thess.* 2:13). Men need to hear a message from God before there is any possibility of holiness in their lives. 'I have written unto you, young men, because you are strong, and the word of God abides in you, and you have overcome the wicked one' (*1 John* 2:14). 'Thy word have I hid in mine heart, that I might not sin against thee' (*Psa.* 119:11).

---

[1] Quoted in my *Wesley and Men Who Followed* (Edinburgh: The Banner of Truth Trust, 2003), p. 172.

Ask a true evangelical how anyone can come to inner peace and spiritual strength, and he or she will say, the Bible has to be the starting point. Put the same question to others and the answers are very different.

One answer we may call the *religious institutions* answer. It tells us that we find God by joining a religious community where salvation is to be found. Belong to that community, be identified with it, listen to its teachers and our spiritual need will be met. This was the answer of the Pharisees. They believed they were the true teachers of holiness, but their teaching was not according to Scripture. It was about such religious devotees that Christ spoke these startling words: 'In vain do they worship me, teaching for doctrines the commandments of men' (*Matt.* 15:9). Today the Roman Catholic Church teaches that the way to holiness is through belonging to her communion, receiving her sacraments, and believing her priests. 'Belong to this Church', it is said, 'and you will belong to Christ; spiritual life will follow.'[1] It was for resisting this teaching that hundreds of believers suffered death at the time of the Reformation.

[1] See the authorised *Catechism of the Catholic Church* (London: Geoffrey Chapman, 1995), pp. 441-2: 'The *ordinary* and universal *Magisterium* of the Pope and the bishops in communion with him teaches the faithful the truth to believe . . . a true *filial spirit towards the Church* . . . is the normal flowering of the baptismal grace which has begotten us in the womb of the Church and made us members of the Body of Christ. In her motherly care the Church grants us the mercy of God.' John Lennon represented a similar faith in institutions when, in 1966, he pronounced the Beatles 'were more popular than Jesus Christ', and went to the ashram of Maharisha Yoga in India. Michael Raiter, *Stirrings of the Soul: Evangelicals and the New Spirituality* (London: Matthias Media, Good Book Company, 2003), pp. 55-7.

The answer of the promoters of the so-called *non-religious 'spirituality'* is equally different from that of the evangelical. They say that peace, serenity, and fulfilment, do not come through any external connection or relationship; they are to be discovered within oneself. Religious institutions are not necessary for anyone to become 'spiritual'. Rather 'ladders' exist within ourselves which can lead us upwards to a higher spiritual state and happiness. Some may refer to that higher state as 'God' or simply as 'the Other'. They say it is the experience, not the words, that matters.

Another term for this kind of teaching is *mysticism*. From the earliest centuries mysticism has challenged Christianity. It takes various forms but the common characteristic is its concern with feelings and experiences rather than with the mind and the understanding. No information from without is necessary; we all have an 'inner light' to follow. If you ask, 'How do you know that "light" will guide you safely?', the answer is, 'Trust your feelings, they will show you.'

It is worth thinking why this teaching receives so much popularity today. For one thing, instead of humbling us, it tells us we already have enough resources to help ourselves. There is no need for us to come under the authority of anyone else. We like being self-centred, and that is just what this thinking encourages us to be.

There is another reason why mysticism is resurgent: it provides a means for lapsed Christians to remain, as they think, 'spiritual' people. Formerly in our nation, Christianity was identified with the acceptance of definite beliefs. A Christian believed the Bible; the Established Church had the 39 Articles and other denominations their Confessions of Faith. But when the Bible and its doctrines came under sustained attack from the world, and revelation of truth from God was denied, the way of retreat that appealed to numbers was to fall back on personal, emotional experience. Mysticism, it was thought, could be an aid to a declining orthodox Christianity.[1]

An example of someone who fell from Christian truth, and yet thought she remained a Christian, is Hannah Pearsall Smith. You may not know the name, but she wrote one of the most popular evangelical books of the Victorian period, *The Christian's Secret of a Happy Life*. In the 1870s she and her husband, Robert Pearsall Smith, came from the United States to England on a mission to teach. They rapidly became influential and were connected with those who began the meetings here in Keswick in 1875. But Hannah Smith's religion was anchored on experiences, not on Scripture, and long before her death she abandoned a profession of evangelical belief and lapsed into a vague kind of mystic universalism. She wrote in 1902:

> In my extreme evangelical days, what I got at was the fact of God's forgiveness, although I hung it on a hook that I had afterwards to discard. . . . The various hooks upon which I hung this fact at the different stages of my progress were entirely immaterial after all. The bottom fact is the only thing. And I fully believe that this bottom fact of a good Creator, can be got at through all sorts of

[1] That even good men fell into this mistake is clear in G. F. Barbour's *Life of Alexander Whyte* (London: Hodder and Stoughton, 1923). Whyte's failure to stand for the full integrity of Scripture coincided with his interest in mysticism, which he said, 'means spirituality of the deepest kind'. On which statement Barbour commented: 'this spirituality he now increasingly found in authors who differed widely from one another, and from the Puritan tradition on which his faith had first been nourished' (p. 381).

religious beliefs and all sorts of religious ceremonies, and that it does not matter what these are, provided the soul is honest in regard to them.[1]

Mysticism is no ally to Christianity. It does not lead to light but to confusion, uncertainty, and darkness. It is wrong from its starting point. The idea of an inner light that can lead us safely to God is a delusion. 'The things of God knoweth no man, but the Spirit of God . . . the natural man receiveth not the things of the Spirit of God: for they are foolishness unto him: neither can he know them, because they are spiritually discerned' (*1 Cor.* 2:11, 14).

The evangelical rightly believes that we cannot find God of ourselves. No civilisation made a greater attempt to do that than did that of ancient Greece, and yet of that civilisation Scripture asserts, 'The world by wisdom knew not God' (*1 Cor.* 1:21). We can only come to know God as he speaks to us, and he speaks to us in his word written. No one builds on rock, Jesus says, except those who hear his words and do them.

3. Evangelical holiness is the result of a new birth. This follows from what has already been said. There is something so seriously wrong in human nature that nothing can correct it except a new beginning, a second birth. Nothing else can change a person's nature—not education, not even joining a church. The change needed in sinners is so great that only God can do it, for it is nothing less than a change from death to life. The new birth is

---

[1] *A Religious Rebel; the Letters of 'H.W.S.',* ed. Logan Pearsall Smith (London: Nisbet, 1949), pp. 149-50. Her husband fell into complete agnosticism. In 1905 she wrote: 'I do wonder if a procession of all the people I have helped will come to meet me when I enter Heaven! Or will they have discovered that I had got everything wrong? . . . It will be rather interesting to see.' *Ibid.,* p. 180.

represented in Scripture as the result of the same power as that which brought the whole creation into being. To be 'born of the Spirit' means nothing less than that 'God, who command-ed the light to shine out of darkness, hath shined in our hearts' (*2 Cor.* 4:6). 'For we are his workmanship, created in Christ Jesus' (*Eph.* 2:10). 'With men it is impossible but not with God' (*Mark* 10:27).

This is why the new birth is such a surprising, wonderful event. It cannot be arranged or predicted; every conversion is the result of the direct intervention of God. In a moment the most improbable of men and women may become new persons by the grace of God. In the eighteenth century William Hone was among the many who despised Christ, but a great change came, and he lived to write the words,

> The proudest heart that ever beat
> Hath been subdued in me:
> The wildest will that ever rose
> To scorn Thy cause, and aid Thy foes,
> Is quelled, my God, by Thee.

The new birth is the only source of personal holiness.

Distinguishing features of evangelical holiness

1. Devotion and Commitment to the Lord Jesus Christ. Jesus told Nicodemus that the result of the new birth is spiritual sight, 'Except a man be born again he cannot see the kingdom of God', but the reborn man enters a new spiritual realm, he can see some-thing he never dreamed of, something that will transform his life forever; he sees 'the glory of God in the face of Jesus Christ'. 'We beheld his glory.' This is what it means to be a Christian. When

Jesus said, 'Everyone who sees the Son, and believes in him' has everlasting life (*John* 6:40), he was not referring to physical sight. Nicodemus at first viewed Jesus as only 'a teacher sent from God'. When he was reborn he saw him as God the Son, the Lord of glory. Nicodemus became a believer because he was reborn. 'By grace are ye saved through faith, and that not of yourselves: it is the gift of God' (*Eph.* 2:8).

Scripture makes clear that devotion to Christ is universal Christian experience. It is necessarily so, because it is the purpose of the Holy Spirit to glorify Christ by creating just such experience. Thus when he illuminates the minds of sinners they begin to see Christ as wonderful, someone worth more to them than all the world. In one of his parables Jesus illustrates becoming a Christian from the business of a dealer in precious stones. One day the dealer finds a pearl of amazing value, and 'he went and sold all that he had, and bought it' (*Matt.* 13:45, 46). That is what happens to a Christian. Now he knows of nothing which can be compared in value with Christ. He can understand why Paul wrote, 'I count all things but loss for the excellency of the knowledge of Christ Jesus my Lord: for whom I have suffered the loss of all things' (*Phil.* 3:8).

This is the work of the Holy Spirit. By nature we are indifferent to Christ, we do not want him to rule over us. In the days of his flesh many saw him and were unmoved; today many can read the Bible and see nothing marvellous in Christ. But when the Spirit of God makes him known, the whole of life must change. When sinners know the love of the Saviour, they know that they owe everything to him. And the inevitable result is gratitude and commitment to Christ. 'To you therefore that believe he is precious'—

more precious than anyone or anything else. Jesus the Lord is worshiped, trusted, obeyed, and loved. This is true evidence of godliness. God loves his Son. When we are made his children we begin to be like God, for now we also love the Son.

We should note what proof this devotion to Christ gives of the truth of the gospel. Mankind is divided into many different races and families; no two could be described as the same: but when anyone becomes a member of the kingdom of God, it does not matter at what date, or where they live, they have the common family likeness, and that likeness is devotion to Christ. A convert in 1510 or 2010 will have a life that revolves round Christ.

A letter from Pliny, the Roman Pro-consul in Asia Minor, to the Emperor Trajan has survived in which he reports that the persecuted Christians of his day met early in the morning and sang praise to Christ as God.[1] That was about the year A.D. 112. But if we go on down through the centuries it is the same song that continues. From the Middle Ages the words we hear are,

> Jesus the very thought of Thee
> With sweetness fills my breast.

At the Reformation the song was louder and multiplied across the nations. In the eighteenth century, German Christians sang,

> When morning gilds the skies,
> My heart awaking cries,
> 'May Jesus Christ be praised!'

In England, at the same date, thousands took up the words of

[1] 'They were accustomed on a certain day to meet before daylight, and to repeat among themselves an hymn to Christ as to a god.' Joseph Milner, *History of the Church of Christ*, vol. 1 (London, 1812), p. 147. Also Pliny, *Letters*, 10:96.

Charles Wesley's hymn 'Jesu, Lover of my soul', with its lines,

> Thou, O Christ, art all I want;
> More than all in Thee I find.

Others sang with John Newton, 'How sweet the name of Jesus sounds'; or in Wales,

> Jesus, Jesus, all sufficient,
> Beyond telling is Thy worth.

The first Hindu convert in India in the 1790s put the very same feelings into verse when he wrote the beautiful hymn that begins,

> O Thou, my soul, forget no more
> The Friend who all thy misery bore;
> Let every idol be forgot,
> But, O my soul, forget Him not.

Or come down to Keswick in the nineteenth century and ask, what is the favourite hymn? It was probably Havergal's,

> Take my life and let it be,
> Consecrated, Lord, to Thee.

This universal experience cannot be explained apart from the truth that it is all the work of one Author. If holiness was something to be acquired by nationality, or by culture, it could never have such a common feature. All born of the Spirit of God have a nature that seeks to advance the glory of Christ. This is evangelical holiness.

2. *Love*. I have already said that love comes from the new birth. This is what Scripture says: 'Love is of God; and every one that loveth is born of God, and knoweth God. He that loveth not knoweth not God; for God is love. . . . Herein is love, not that

we loved God, but that he loved us, and sent his Son to be the propitiation for our sins' (*1 John* 4:7, 8, 10). Love is the consequence of the indwelling of God, for the very nature of God is love. It is love that prompts the life of the Christian. Faith *receives* and love *works*. Love is the dynamic in a Christian; it energises and inspires. In proportion to his love the believer will be zealous and fervent; ready to serve; ready, if needs be, to suffer. 'Love beareth all things, believeth all things, hopeth all things, endureth all things. Love never faileth' (*1 Cor.* 13:7, 8) 'Many waters cannot quench love, neither can the floods drown it' (*Song of Sol.* 8:7).

For a picture of this evangelical love we cannot do better than go into the house of Simon the Pharisee where Jesus is the guest. On that day something was seen in that home which had never been seen before. A woman had found her way in; 'a sinner' says the Scripture; and while Simon gave Jesus no water with which to wash his feet, she began to wash them with tears, to wipe them with her hair, and to anoint them. The Lord gives us the explanation: it was because she was forgiven much that she loved much. Simon did nothing for Christ because he had never known that forgiveness. No sinner loves until he has first experienced God's love. 'We love him, because he first loved us' (*1 John* 4:19), or, in the words of Toplady's hymn,

> Loved of my God, for Him again,
> With zeal intense I'd burn.

Evangelical history is full of the same kind of people as the woman in Simon's house. William Tyndale was persecuted and finally put to death in 1536 for translating the Scriptures into English. Listen how he wrote to his persecutors:

If we be in Christ, we work for no worldly purpose, but of love: as Paul saith, *2 Cor.* 5, 'The love of Christ compelleth us.' We are otherwise minded than when Peter drew his sword to fight for Christ. We are ready to suffer with Christ, and to lose life and all for our very enemies, to bring them unto Christ. . . . Christ is all to a Christian man. Christ is the cause why I love thee, why I am ready to do the utmost of my power for thee, and why I pray for thee. And as long as the cause abides, so long lasts the effect: even as it is always day so long as the sun shineth. Do therefore the worst thou canst unto me, take away my goods, take away my good name; yet as long as Christ remaineth in my heart, so long I love thee not a whit the less, and so long art thou as dear unto me as mine own soul. . . . Thine unkindness compared unto His kindness is nothing at all; yea, it is swallowed up as a little smoke of a mighty wind, and is no more thought upon.[1]

Christian women through the ages have acted in the same spirit. Many of them have been at the Keswick Convention. In the year 1887 thirty young people at the Convention volunteered for missionary service. A fund was launched to help them, and the first to be supported was Amy Carmichael. She was a talented young woman in her early twenties who could have spent her days living a comfortable life in beautiful Cumbria. Instead she gave herself to the needy women and children of India. By 1906 she had built a 'family' of 70 such individuals at Dohnavur; in 1913 the number was 130, and by the time her long service ended

---

[1] *Works of William Tyndale* (repr. Edinburgh: The Banner of Truth Trust, 2010) vol. 1, pp. 297-8. Thomas Adam wrote: 'The further a man advances in Christianity, the more he sees the ignorance, selfish baseness, and corruption of mankind; and yet the more he loves them. The wisdom from above can account for this impossibility.' *Private Thoughts*, p. 190.

in 1951, the number was 900. It is a remarkable record and the explanation lies in her words of prayer, 'Lord, do Thou turn me all into love, and all my love into obedience, and let my obedience be without interruption.'[1] In poetry she wrote,

> O Love revealed at Calvary,
> Thy glory lights eternity.

Faced with the miseries to be seen in India, she was sure, 'Cruelty and wrong are not the greatest forces in the world. There is nothing eternal in them. Only love is eternal.' The secret of her work was summed up by one who knew her in the words, 'Dear Amma—she never understood how the love of God within her was so powerful a magnet that all through her life others were drawn irresistibly to her.'[2]

Another early visitor here at Keswick was Hudson Taylor. When once asked how he explained the great missionary advance in China, he replied, 'Love first, then suffering, then a deeper love—thus only can God's work be done.'[3]

Biblical holiness is the effect of the love of Christ constraining men and women to live for him, and love can do what nothing else can do. When evangelical belief was being sneered at in the nineteenth century, Joseph Parker wrote,

[1] This prayer, originally that of Jeremy Taylor, was said to be 'always hers'. Elisabeth Elliot, *A Chance to Die: The life and legacy of Amy Carmichael* (Grand Rapids: Fleming Revell, 1987), p. 151.

[2] Frank Houghton, *Amy Carmichael of Dohnavur* (London: SPCK, 1953), p. 105. See also p. 219.

[3] Howard and Geraldine Taylor, *Hudson Taylor in Early Years* (London: CIM, 1932), p. 291.

These may be old-fashioned doctrines, but they created missionary societies, hospitals, orphanages, and refuges of penitence; they gave every child a new value, every father a new responsibility, every mother a new hope, and constituted human society into a new conscience and a new trust.[1]

3. *Humility*. There is a great paradox in the Christian life. The Christian is a son of God, an heir of glory, and a possessor of eternal life; he knows God in Christ, and has begun to be like him. Yet far from being proud of himself, he thinks very differently about himself than the way he used to think before he was a Christian. In the presence of God he knows he is an unworthy sinner, and the more he knows Christ the less he thinks of himself. Isaac Watts captured evangelical experience when he wrote the lines

> The more Thy glories strike mine eyes,
>   The humbler I shall lie:
> Thus while I sink, my joys shall rise
>   Unmeasurably high.[2]

The language of a Christian is 'not I but Christ', and the more he knows Christ, the more he mourns his weak love, his poor faith, his small usefulness. 'O wretched man that I am', he can say from his heart. Daily he has reason to be ashamed. He goes on repenting all his days, and will die dependent on the mercy of God. 'Less than the least of all saints', 'the chief of sinners', is Paul's estimate of himself.

And yet, here is the paradox, the more the Christian learns this about himself, the happier he is. For the word of Jesus is true:

[1] *A Preacher's Life, An Autobiography of Joseph Parker* (London: Hodder and Stoughton, 1899), p. 99.

[2] The hymn begins, 'Father, I long, I faint to see'.

'Blessed are the poor in spirit: for theirs is the kingdom of God' (*Matt.* 5:3). An old evangelical leader in Wales affirmed, 'We are never nearer to God than when we are lowest in our own estimation.'[1] 'To this man will I look, even to him that is poor and of a contrite spirit, and trembles at my word' (*Isa.* 66:2).

Read the biographies of Christians and it will be seen that evangelical holiness has always had this characteristic. John Calvin wrote, 'Where we see pride, there let us be assured Christ is not known.'[2] George Whitefield, seen by others as a great evangelist, only a few years before his death prayed 'to begin to begin to be a Christian'.[3] William Grimshaw, one of the greatest evangelists to be given to England, died with the words, 'Here goes an unprofitable servant.' John Wesley after a lifetime of service, wrote, 'I have been wandering up and down between fifty and sixty years, endeavouring in my poor way, to do a little good to my fellow men. . . . I can see nothing which I have done or suffered, that will bear looking at. I have no other plea than this,

> I the chief of sinners am
> But Jesus died for me.'

Spurgeon asked his students, 'Do you not wish to hide your head when you contrast yourself with your Lord? We are far, far, far below the true glory of the Well-beloved, and even fall short of our poor idea of him.'[4]

---

[1] *Thomas Charles' Spiritual Counsels,* ed. Edward Morgan (repr. Edinburgh: The Banner of Truth Trust, 1993).

[2] *Commentaries on Philippians, Colossians and Thessalonians* (Edinburgh; Calvin Translation Soc., 1851), p. 93.

[3] *Works of George Whitefield* (London, 1771), vol. 3, p. 343.

[4] *The Sword and the Trowel*, 1880 (London: Passmore and Alabaster), p. 318.

Amy Carmichael comforted herself and others with these words, 'Our dear Lord cares for the broken pieces of our lives, the fragments of all we meant to do, the little that we have to gather up and offer, and He will use even these fragments.'[1]

A sure test whether holiness is genuine or false is whether it exalts or humbles. It is never the work of the Holy Spirit to magnify men. Holiness does not lead anyone to promote self and to talk about self. A. A. Hodge has written about evangelical holiness in a woman in his congregation in Virginia, where he served for six years. She was a woman who, he wrote,

> seemed always to walk on the verge of heaven. I never heard her speak of any one particular of her character or of her own graces. I have come out of the pulpit when the congregation has gone, and have found her upon her knees in her pew, absolutely unconscious of all external objects, so far was she absorbed in worship. When I roused her from her trance, she cried instantly, 'Is He not holy? Is He not glorious? Is He not beautiful? Is He not infinite?' She did not speak of her own love, or of her feelings.[2]

Communion with God by the Holy Spirit

Many years after the death of Christ, the Apostle John affirmed, 'Truly our fellowship is with the Father, and with his Son Jesus Christ' (1 John 1:3). Here is the great mystery which Christ's disciples at first could not understand. When Jesus, at the last supper in the upper room, told them he was going away, and that this would be better for them, they were only dismayed. They did not understand that his going away did not mean that he was going to

[1] Amy Carmichael, *Edges of His Ways* (London: SPCK, 1964), p. 177.
[2] *Evangelical Theology* (Edinburgh: The Banner of Truth Trust, 1990), p. 307.

leave them. On the contrary, he said, he was going in order to be with them always and everywhere. He would send the Holy Spirit, but not as a substitute for himself, for in the Godhead Christ and the Holy Spirit are one. So he can say, 'I will send him unto you', and not contradict himself with the promise, 'I will come to you' (*John* 16:7; 14:18). The purpose of this coming is for a fellowship closer than the disciples could ever know when Jesus was bodily in their midst.

This is a very large subject and I only want to take up one practical question: How is this fellowship with Christ and the Holy Spirit maintained and continued in the lives of Christians? The answer is through the Scriptures. In the upper room Jesus emphasised the fundamental place of his words: 'If a man love me, he will keep my words' (*John* 14:23). 'If ye abide in me and my words abide in you . . .' (15:7). 'Remember the word that I said unto you' (15:20). But how can we hear Christ's words today? The answer is the Holy Spirit. According to Christ's promise, the Spirit of truth has come and given us the very words of Christ. They are in our hands now. 'All Scripture is given by inspiration of God.' The Bible is not simply the thought of God, it is his word: 'We have received, not the spirit of the world, but the Spirit who is of God, that we might know the things that have been freely given to us by God. These things also we speak, not in words which man's wisdom teaches, but which the Holy Spirit teaches. . . . We have the mind of Christ' (*1 Cor.* 2:12, 13, 16).

Communion with God rests on the ongoing teaching ministry of the Holy Spirit by his word. To this Christ refers in his words of intercession: 'I have given them thy word . . . sanctify them through thy truth; thy word is truth' (*John* 17:14, 17). It is not the simple reading of Scripture that sanctifies, but God speaking by his word: 'Take the sword of the Spirit, which is the word of God' (*Eph.* 6:17). William Cowper's words are exactly true:

> The Spirit breathes upon the word,
> And brings the truth to sight;
> Precepts and promises afford
> A sanctifying light.

By this means the believer knows communion with Christ. It is by the Holy Spirit and his word that there is an ongoing receiving from the fullness that is in Christ our head, so that the Christian can repeat the words: 'We beheld his glory, full of grace and truth. . . . And of his fullness have all we received, and grace for grace' (*John* 1:14, 16). 'We all, with open face, beholding as in a glass the glory of the Lord, are changed into the same image from glory to glory, even as by the Spirit of the Lord' (*2 Cor.* 3:18). Such experience is not to be understood apart from Scripture. In the words of an old Methodist:

> Prayer is very good, and there's no gettin' on without that, but I don't believe prayer is prayer without the word. Prayer is no good without faith, and faith cometh by the word of God. I know 'tis so with me. I can't pray right till I get hold of a promise; then I can go so bold as a lion. Prayer without the word is a heartless kind o' thing. There isn't any grip about it.[1]

Ephesians 3:16-21 is a key passage on the relation of faith to the experience of Christ. Paul prays for the Christians at Ephesus, that the Father 'would grant you, according to the riches of his

---

[1] M. G. Pearse, *Daniel Quorn and his Religious Notions* (London: Methodist Conference Office, 1876), pp. 115-6.

glory, to be strengthened with might by his Spirit in the inner man'. For what purpose does he ask for the Spirit's empowering? It is 'that Christ may dwell in your hearts by faith'. The prayer is not that Christ would come to live in them (which was already true), but that the Spirit of God would so strengthen their faith that Christ's indwelling would be a greater conscious reality. And as that happens, they will advance in apprehending the fullness that is in Christ—'that you, being rooted and grounded in love, may be able to comprehend with all saints what is the breadth, and length, and depth, and height; and to know the love of Christ, which passes knowledge, that you might be filled with all the fullness of God'.[1]

It ought to be no secret why evangelicals make so much of the Bible. Why do we read it every day? It is because here Christ meets us, feeds us, and shows himself to be 'the author and finisher of our faith'.

Those who do not know the Holy Spirit talk about 'views of the Bible' as though it were all a matter of different theories. The idea of anyone laying down their life for Scripture is beyond their comprehension. They are puzzled that evangelicals make such a fuss, as they think, about the Bible. They do not understand that real communion with God is by the ministry of the Spirit of truth, through the Holy Scriptures. All the joys and blessings of evangelical holiness are bound up with the truth of Scripture. If the Old Testament believer can say, 'The law of thy

---

[1] As Andrew Bonar wrote: 'This is not any second conversion, but is the Spirit breathing through the heart in a new degree . . . if any make this something by itself, instead of just the Spirit bringing in more of Christ, they are in great danger of mysticism'. *Diary and Life,* (Edinburgh: The Banner of Truth Trust, 2013), p. 256.

mouth is better unto me than thousands of gold and silver' (*Psa.* 119:72), how much more can we with all Scripture before us! The Bible means more to the life of a Christian than the very sun that shines in the sky. Amy Carmichael listed three things upon which the life and blessing of the family at Dohnavur depended, and we are not surprised that she put first 'the verbal inspiration of the Scriptures'.[1]

Much has been said and written on how the Christian grows in holiness. We should avoid all stereotyped answers to that question. There are wide differences in Christian experience, for the Holy Spirit deals with us all individually and personally.[2] But a principle is true for every Christian: it is that grace in Christ is received in proportion to our growth in knowledge of him. Which is another way of saying that godliness will rise as Scripture is understood and obeyed. For that reason the repeated prayer in the Psalm which deals most fully with the believer and holiness, is the prayer for 'teaching' and 'understanding' (*Psa.* 119:33, 34, *etc.*). Matthew Henry was not wrong when he wrote, 'What is it to be sanctified, but to be of God's mind?' That being so, the word of God stands alone as the channel of grace to us. An act of complete surrender to Christ has been represented as the secret of the life of holiness, but our will acts as moved by the light of Christ in our minds, and so the surrender and the holiness must be progressive, for light is

---

[1] Elliot, *Chance to Die,* p. 272.

[2] 'Now I perceived that God dispenses His favours when and how He pleases; that He suits His dispensations to our several states and wants.' A. J. Gordon, quoting a disciple of Charles Simeon, *The Twofold Life* (London: Hodder and Stoughton, 1886), p. 231.

progressively received, and the petition 'that I might know him' will remain the Christian's until 'one sight of Jesus as he is will strike all sin forever dead'.

The greatest disaster that ever happened to the churches of Britain was when the teaching entered that you can live without dependence on the truth of the word of God and not lose the presence of the Holy Spirit. The testimony of Scripture, and of all history, is that when reverence for the word of God goes, then prayer goes, joy goes, holiness goes, and Christ himself goes.

Dangers for evangelical holiness

It is one thing to say that the Bible is the standard to which evangelicals adhere, and another to suppose we adhere to that standard, and understand it as we ought to do. While we ought to prize evangelical history, that does not mean we should close our eyes to defects in the past or present. I turn then to dangers that have occurred in the past and are not unknown in the present.

1. The danger of underestimating the momentous nature of the new birth. Eric Alexander has written: 'I am sure that one of the reasons people are looking for additional, secondary thrills offered at some future stage in their religious experience is that they have devalued the initial work of grace.'[1] This mistake has sometimes been pervasive among evangelicals. What happens at conversion has been treated as though the rebirth only deals with the forgiveness of sin, and that another experience is necessary before a 'victorious Christian life' can be enjoyed. According to this thinking a person can be a believer and still be 'carnal', or

[1] Eric J. Alexander, *Our Great God and Saviour* (Edinburgh: The Banner of Truth Trust, 2010), p.72.

worldly.[1] It is said that someone may know Jesus as Saviour but not yet as Lord and Master.

One aspect of this teaching is right. Conversion is the starting not the finishing point. No one is reborn as a mature Christian. We all begin as spiritual babes. If that was not true many texts would be meaningless. 'Let us press on to maturity . . . Add to your faith . . . Go on being filled with the Spirit' is the language of Scripture (*Heb.* 6:1; *2 Pet.* 1:5; *Eph.* 5:18). But the teaching is wrong because it diminishes the stupendous character of the new birth. Nothing greater will ever happen to us in this life than the point at which we come to possess Christ, and are united with him in eternal life. That happens at the rebirth. 'This is the record, that God has given to us eternal life, and this life is in his Son. He that has the Son of God has the life' (*1 John* 5:11, 12). To be born of God means nothing less than having the life of the Son of God within us. The permanent indwelling of the Spirit of Christ is not a post-conversion experience to which only some believers attain. It is of all Christians that Scripture asserts: 'You are not in the flesh but in the Spirit, if indeed the Spirit of God dwells in you. But if anyone does not have the Spirit of Christ he does not belong to him'—'is none of his' (*Rom.* 8:9).

The teaching of the New Testament is not that God brings us to conversion and that later we may come to sanctification. Rather, it is that once a person is born again the very life of Christ is in that person, and their complete salvation is already a certainty.

[1] This has been mistakenly based on words of Paul in *1 Cor.* 3:3. 'There is no delusion more inexcusable, because none is more directly opposed to every doctrine of the Bible, than the idea that a state of grace is consistent with a life of sin.' Charles Hodge, *The Way of Life* (London: The Banner of Truth Trust, 1959), p. 219.

The saving work of God never stops short of glorification (*Rom.* 8:30). Therefore Paul can say to the believers at Philippi, 'that he which has begun a good work in you will perform it until the day of Jesus Christ' (*Phil.* 1:6).

Certainly the holiness of the Christian is imperfect, and far from complete, but already the believer has a new nature and a glorious change has begun that will lead to full conformity to Christ in glory.

It is a serious error to believe that a worldly-living person can be a true Christian. As a consequence of that error the unregenerate have too often been given a false assurance of salvation and admitted into the membership of churches. When that happens churches have to lower their standards to accommodate the tastes of the worldly, and before long what distinguishes the church from the world begins to disappear. The church is called to be as salt in the world, keeping society from utter putrefaction; but, says our Lord, if the salt becomes tasteless, 'It is no longer good for anything, except to be thrown out and trampled underfoot by men' (*Matt.* 5:13). That, in a sentence, is the history of all churches whenever their membership and holiness part company. What John Wesley said of the Methodists applies equally to all evangelical churches:

> I am not afraid that the people called Methodists should ever cease
> ... But I am afraid, lest they should only exist as a dead sect, having the form of religion without the power. And this undoubtedly will be the case, unless they hold fast both the doctrine, spirit, and discipline with which they first set out.[1]

[1] Luke Tyerman, *Life and Times of John Wesley* (London: Hodder and Stoughton, 1890), vol. 3, p. 519. The standard for membership in Methodist Societies was high.

2. The danger of wrongly relating the objective and the subjective.
A difference of opinion has repeatedly occurred among evangelicals on this point. It concerns what proportion of emphasis should be given to the objective and to the subjective when we speak of sanctification. By the term 'objective' we refer to things outside our personal experience and consciousness. It is an objective fact that whether we are here or not, this building is on Skiddaw Street in Keswick. But should you feel a headache this morning that is true of no one but yourself; it is your subjective experience. The death and resurrection of Christ are objective facts—they took place in history outside our experience. But such things as prayer, meditation, and self-discipline, are subjective— we have an inner consciousness of them; they are experiences in which we are involved.

This distinction has vital relevance to the understanding of evangelical holiness. For the Christian, is holiness objective or subjective? That is a crucial question. And the answer of Scripture is that *it is both,* and if we do not see both, and in their right relationship to the other, our understanding is going to be defective.

Take the subjective first. Many Christian duties come under this heading. The Christian is to believe, to abide in Christ, to give all diligence to growth in grace, to watch and pray, to feed on the word of God, and much more. The Christian life is not some Quietist, passive waiting for God to do something for us. It requires energy, action, effort. We are to 'fight the good fight of faith' (*1 Tim.* 6:12).

This is stressed in the New Testament teaching on sanctification. There is a stirring call to the believer to be engaged in the earnest and lifelong pursuit of holiness. The Apostle Paul's practice is unmistakable in this regard. He pursues holiness, and says, 'Not as though I had already attained, either were already perfect' (*Phil.* 3:12); 'So fight I, not as one that beats the air: but I keep under my body' (*1 Cor.* 9:26, 27).

We ignore the subjective at our peril. We are commanded to examine ourselves whether Christ is in us (*2 Cor.* 13:5), and we are warned, 'Follow holiness, without which no man shall see the Lord' (*Heb.* 12:14). Any teaching which says we must only look at Christ, not at ourselves, is not from the New Testament. It is possible to hold Christ as an article of faith and yet not to know communion with him. Such was the case of the foolish virgins; they had lamps but no oil in them; they professed to be waiting for the bridegroom but the door was shut against them when he came. There are subjective tests to be applied to confirm we are genuine believers: 'And hereby do we know that we know him, if we keep his commandments. He that says, I know him, and keeps not his commandments, is a liar and the truth is not in him' (*1 John* 2:3, 4). Or again, it is not enough to believe in the second coming of Christ. I need to ask myself, Do I 'love his appearing'? Do I prepare for it, as Scripture says every Christian will do, 'Every man that has this hope in him purifies himself, even as he is pure' (*1 John* 3:3).[1]

Yet while all this is vital teaching, the New Testament does not begin with the subjective. Rather it tells us that the first thing the Christian needs to understand is the objective. And the objective includes this amazing fact: regardless of what the weakest

---

[1] This is not to say that our assurance of salvation is to be based on our sanctification; yet the Scripture teaches that any who believes he is a Christian, without an evidence of Christ's work in him, is self-deluded.

believers feel about themselves, they are already said to be holy. That is the repeated biblical description of every believer. The church at Corinth are 'those that have been sanctified in Christ Jesus'. All the Christians to whom Paul writes, whether at Ephesus, Philippi, or wherever, have a common title. They are 'the saints in Christ Jesus'. He is not saying that they are going to become 'saints'. It was already true, and it was true for this reason, they were 'in Christ'.

This is the repeated New Testament assertion about Christians. What does 'in Christ' mean? The meaning is not to be defined solely in terms of our experience because Scripture says this relationship of Christians to Christ has its origin long before they were even born. They were in Christ, Paul asserts, 'before the foundation of the world' (*Eph.* 1:4). They were in Christ when Jesus died at Calvary. 'You have died', the Scripture says to believers (*Col.* 3:3). How can living people be said to have died? Was Paul referring to an experience which they could remember having? No, he was not. In the purpose of God, they died when Christ died in their place. It was because of that union that Jesus suffered. 'I am crucified with Christ' is not an experience we are to seek; it was accomplished for me when Jesus died. 'Christ was once offered to bear the sins of many' (*Heb.* 9:28).

The doctrine of union with Christ is the basis for the truth of what evangelicals believe about justification. 'There is therefore now no condemnation to them that are in Christ Jesus' (*Rom.* 8:1). Believers are dead to the penalty of God's law, for Jesus has met every claim in their place. But union with Christ is no less the basis of sanctification. Believers have union with Christ not only in his death but in his life. To be 'in Christ' is to have the secure title for complete salvation. Christ will be everything for those with whom he is united. So to the Christians at Corinth the apostle writes, 'Of him are you in Christ Jesus, who of God is made unto us wisdom, and righteousness, and sanctification, and redemption' (*1 Cor.* 1:30). He is not saying this is true because you have experienced all these things. They had not. 'Redemption' refers to the resurrection of the body and to final glorification in the likeness of Christ. That was still in the future. But because they were 'in Christ' he says it already belonged to them.

It is vitally important that the priority which the New Testament gives to the objective comes first. Because:

(1.) If what Christ has done for us is not kept first, *the pursuit of holiness can easily cease to be evangelical.* 'Evangelical' means 'good news'. Any teaching on holiness which puts the main emphasis on the Christian's duty, turns sanctification into a matter of self-effort, a work dependent on ourselves, or an experience we have to seek. If that were the case it would not be good news. Grace would fall into the second place and our works be put before the grace of God.[1]

---

[1] John Downame speaks for Puritan thought when he writes: 'The efficient cause motivating us to perform all the duties of a godly life, ought to be the love of God, which is the fountain of true obedience, and should be so powerful in us that we should thereby be moved to serve, like children, our heavenly Father.' *A Guide to Godliness* (London, 1629), p. 420. A. J. Gordon is not always a sure guide, but we think he is correct when he writes: 'It seems to us that the old Puritan writers held together these two sides of truth, and preserved their balance to a remarkable degree. They expounded most clearly the objective work of Christ, and they also upheld his subjective work, with a minuteness and a depth of insight quite beyond anything we witness in our day.' *The Twofold Life*, p. 217. This is not to say there are not differences of emphases among the Puritans, for example, as between Walter Marshall's *Gospel Mystery of Sanctification* (1692) and Jonathan Edwards' *Religious*

This is not an imaginary danger. In the eighteenth century in England there were clergy who lamented the moral decline and spoke and wrote about holiness. One of them was William Law, who wrote *A Serious Call to a Devout and Holy Life* (1729). Yet the teaching of these men brought no change to the church and the nation. It was because it was not evangelical; they directed non-Christians to live as though they were Christians. It was only when Whitefield, the Wesleys, and others began to preach Christ, the necessity of the Holy Spirit and the new birth that a real and mighty change began. The advance of real Christianity is always led by the recovery of the great objective evangelical truths:

> Not what I feel or do
>   Can give me peace with God;
> Not all my prayers, and sighs and tears
>   Can bear my awful load.
>
> Thy love to me, O God,
>   Not mine, O Lord, to Thee,
> Can rid me of this dark unrest,
>   And set my spirit free.

Someone may ask, whether putting this stress on the objective is not a denial of what I have said earlier. I said there are many things we are commanded to do—to watch, to pray, to fight. That is right; but the great reason why the Christian is to follow after holiness is because of what is already true for him. His growth in grace is not to gain acceptance with God. He is already free from condemnation. He does not practise holiness to win the love of God.

Affections (1746). Both are classic evangelical volumes, the authors of which were addressing different needs in different locations.

That love has already come to him. Christ himself has already come to him, and lives in him by his Spirit. The very weakest member of Christ is the temple of the Holy Spirit. This is the great motive for sanctification, stated so clearly by the apostle: 'Work out your own salvation with fear and trembling. For it is God who is at work in you both to will and to do for his good pleasure' (*Phil.* 2:13).

I do not believe in holy buildings, but have we not all sometimes been in a great cathedral where all is silent and we have felt the need to walk quietly and to speak softly? But Christ in me, God in me, is the astonishing reason why a Christian should live in a certain way. How can I do otherwise if I believe that all my life is being spent in the very presence of God?

So the New Testament's call to holiness, in essence, is a call to Christians to 'be what you are'. 'Abide in him'—that is to say, Stay where you are! You are in him: now consciously remain believing in him; live in the realization that you are in Christ and Christ in you. Such was the final exhortation of the Apostle John, 'And now little children, abide in him' (*1 John* 2:28).

(2.) There is a second reason why the objective needs to be kept first. Where that ceases to be the case *the tendency comes in to give undue importance to feelings and emotion in the Christian life.* Of course, feelings have a place; joy and love and peace are among God-given blessings. But to live by faith in Christ is not the same as to live by feelings. Spurgeon has related an occasion when he was visiting a member of his congregation who was dying from a debilitating disease. Spurgeon counselled the man that in his great weakness his spirits were bound to fall, but he must not think that his faith was giving way. 'Do not be cast down by your feelings', he told him. To which the man at once replied, 'No, sir, I am in no danger of that, for when I have had the most joyful feelings, I never rested in them. You have taught me that a soul can only lean on eternal verities, and these I know come from the mouth of God, and never from the changing feelings of the flesh.' Spurgeon was thankful for such a response and, in reporting it to others, he added, 'Yes, that is it. Do not rise upon feelings, and you will not sink under them. Keep to believing: rest all your weight upon the promises of God, and when heart and flesh fail, God will be the strength of your heart and your portion for ever.'[1]

Wherever evangelical teaching has been strongest, this emphasis has been kept to the front.[2] In the last days of the life of Dr Martyn Lloyd-Jones there were no lines he quoted more often than the words of the hymn

> My hope is built on nothing less
>   Than Jesu's blood and righteousness:
> I dare not trust the sweetest frame,
>   But wholly lean on Jesu's name.
>   *On Christ, the Solid Rock, I stand:*
>   *All other ground is sinking sand.*

---

[1] *The Sword and the Trowel*, 1883, p. 231.

[2] Richard Sibbes, the Puritan leader, writes that God 'knows whom to cheer up, and when and in what degree, and to what purpose and service; and remember always that these enlargements of spirit are as occasional refreshings in the way, not daily food to live upon. We maintain our life by faith, not by sight or feeling.' *Works* (repr. Edinburgh: The Banner of Truth Trust, 2001), vol. 5, p. 443. 'It is a mistake very injurious to us to set our *feelings* of comfort, or of no comfort, as our ground and rule in our communion with God, instead of the *word* of truth.' *Thomas Charles' Spiritual Counsels*, p. 445. 'I had great comfort from the remark of a brother who said, "It was impossible for God's people to please him better in any way, than by *trusting* him." Religion should not be a *rapture*, but a *habit*.' *Select Remains of William Nevins* (New York: Taylor, 1836), pp. 56, 386.

This is what we are taught in Scripture. The Apostle John wrote, 'I heard a voice from heaven saying unto me, write, Blessed are the dead that die in the Lord.' What makes them 'blessed', happy? One thing alone: not what they may be feeling, but that they are 'in the Lord' (*Rev.* 14:13).

3. The danger of allowing the contemporary culture to affect our standards for Christian living. This is far too large a theme to permit anything more than a short reference to it here. But it is a subject which needs urgent attention.

Let me read you the words of Ronald Knox in which he describes a typical evangelical household at the beginning of the twentieth century. It was a way of living, he wrote, which had 'external marks, a strong devotion to and belief in Scripture; a careful observance of Sunday; framed texts, family prayers, and something indefinably patriarchal about the ordering of the household.'[1]

Now in connection with these marks it would be profitable to consider why several of them are not so prominent among evangelicals today. Is devotion to Scripture and hunger for Scripture as strong as it used to be? Are the numbers listening to the exposition of Scripture on Sunday evenings in our churches what they used to be? There is reason to doubt it. Some of you will remember here at Keswick years ago how the evening service was taken up mainly by two sessions of preaching from the word of God. I was reading the other day an address by Kenneth Prior

---

[1] David Rooney, *The Wine of Certitude: A Literary Biography of Ronald Knox* (San Francisco; Ignatius Press, 2009), p. 39, where he quotes from Knox's autobiography, *A Spiritual Aeneid.* The faith of Knox's father, which the son turned from, will be found in Edmund A. Knox, *Reminiscences of an Octogenarian, 1847-1934* (London: Hutchinson, 1935).

at the Convention in 1963. He expressed his concern that some evangelicals were beginning to confuse listening to Scripture with entertainment, and wanted funny stories and illustrations more than serious thought.[1] That tendency has increased.

And what of prayer? Here at Keswick in 1963 the number attending the 7 a.m. prayer meetings was given as between one and two thousand. Is conviction on the place of prayer stronger or weaker in our churches today than it was then? Are family prayers still the mark of evangelical households? It was not a Victorian institution. Long before that era, daily family prayer was a mark of Christian homes in Britain.[2] Along with Joshua, evangelicals resolved, 'As for me and my house, we will serve the Lord.'

Then what of the other mark of evangelicals that Knox mentioned, 'a careful observance of Sunday'? Some regard differences of opinion over the observance of the Lord's day as simply a permissible change in customs. I think the Scriptures teach it is much more than that. One day in seven was specially set apart by God at the creation. It was made, not for the Jew, but for mankind. And it is not only the fourth commandment that is seldom heard among us; we hear little today of all Ten. Once the Ten Commandments were seen on the walls of many churches, and taught in our schools. Today the Commandments are very much

[1] *The Keswick Week 1963* (London: Marshall, Morgan & Scott), p. 147. With reference to decline in concern for biblical truth Mr Prior also instanced, 'Christian bookshops have been having a very thin time; most of them have been driven off the main high streets in most cities' (p. 149).

[2] John Flavel wrote to the people of Dartmouth in 1671: 'Set up, I beseech you, the ancient and comfortable duties of reading the Scriptures, singing of psalms and prayer, in all your dwelling places. And do these things conscientiously, as men that have to do with God.' *Works of John Flavel* (repr. Edinburgh, The Banner of Truth Trust, 1997), vol. 1, p. 29.

in the background in many churches, if they are referred to at all. This change can only mean there is a reduced concern about sin. For it is the law of God that defines sin; it is the law that proves we have no hope in ourselves: 'I had not known sin', says Paul, 'but by the law' (*Rom.* 7:7). Is the exceeding sinfulness of sin still a mark of evangelicals today?

Time demands that I over-simplify this subject, but my point is that the areas of contemporary evangelical weakness correspond to the areas where the pressure of non-Christian culture has got into our lives. We are in the age of entertainment and sound-bites. It is a diet that requires no effort, just a moment to switch it on. Never a word will it tell us about delighting 'in the law of the Lord' and meditating in it 'day and night' (*Psa.* 1:2). And what does our society tell us about sin and the Ten Commandments? Nothing at all, unless it is to tell us that such words belong to an age when life was dismal and repressive.

Man stands opposed to authority and revelation. Sin is therefore a very unpopular subject. This is not new. In the 1960s the Keswick Convention was accused of being a 'sombre' place because of the attention given to sin. Today the word is rarely to be heard. There is surely reason to fear we are being pressured into the world's mould. Being 'relevant' has often come to mean not offending the tastes of the world. We are concerned that our churches should be successful, and too easily assume that concessions to the spirit of the age will help to that end. After all, how can the gospel spread unless we make it popular?[1] And how can it be popular if we say things that our contemporaries so dislike?

---

[1] The rush for contemporary music in the worship of the church has been one consequence of this concern. I address that subject below, pp. 89-94.

I believe that when the history of modern evangelicalism is set down it will record that our weakness was connected with the degree to which beliefs and practices were compromised. Because the motive may be good—that is, to gain influence for the gospel—the danger is not seen. In essence it is the sin of being concerned to please men, and to forget the Holy Spirit 'whom God has given to those who obey him' (*Acts* 5:32).

I leave with you the case of a church you all know. In that church were found a man and his wife who sold their property and gave a sum of money to the church. They said the sum donated was all they had received from the sale; but it was not. They were not under any obligation to give the whole amount to the church, but as church members they were under obligation to keep the ninth commandment and to tell the truth. Is it so serious to lie? Yes, the Bible says, liars do not enter heaven. Well, as you know, the leader in this church was Simon Peter. Acting on Scripture, he rebuked the man and his wife in turn, telling them they had not lied to men but to God. Both fell down dead. What happened next? People did not come rushing with flowers to express their sympathy. Instead, Luke tells us, 'Great fear came over all the church, and over all who heard these things . . . and none of the rest dared associate with them' (*Acts* 5: 11, 13).

Here was a case where the bold reproof of sin alarmed the public. Is the rebuking of sin a natural way to promote gospel success? It is not, and yet that is what happened because God is not dependent on the natural: 'And all the more believers in the Lord, multitudes of men and women, were constantly added.' The fear of God is not only the beginning of wisdom, it should be the beginning of evangelism. At the end of his long life, John

Wesley said:

> I never heard or read of any considerable revival of religion, which was not attended with a spirit of reproving. Thus it was in England, when the present revival of religion began about fifty years ago. All the subjects of that revival,—all the Methodists, in every place,—were reprovers of outward sin.[1]

The calling of Christians is to be faithful, not popular. Commonly it is when those who love the Saviour stand apart from the world that they are most used to be a blessing to it. Surely the subject of evangelical holiness goes to the heart of present need. We need more deliverance from the fear of man, more commitment to the word of God, and more love for our fellow sinners. In a word, we need a fresh outpouring of the Spirit of God. May these three weeks at Keswick in the summer of 2010 find many of us praying more earnestly for a change in ourselves and in our churches!

[1] Tyerman, *Wesley*, vol. 3, p. 563. We all know that a rebuke insensitively spoken can do more harm than good. But a duty misused is no argument for it not to be practised at all. Our culture is for the charitable toleration of good and bad, truth and error. The main reason for our silence is the fear of man, and our lack of greater love. We may not agree with all that the late Mrs Mary Whitehouse said, but the impact of her words on social behaviour was considerable.

2

THE ATTACK ON THE BIBLE[1]

Professor A. J. P. Taylor of Oxford, in his volume *English History 1914-1945,* writes of the decline of belief in Christianity which had taken place in Britain by the 1920s. One statement stands out especially in what he says. He goes back over a thousand years before he finds an alteration in national life which he thinks equally momentous. The decline of Christianity, he says, was a change 'as great a happening as any in English history since the conversion of the Anglo Saxons to Christianity'. And what caused such a great change? He lists 'the higher criticism which discredited the verbal inspiration of the Bible—a hard knock especially against Protestantism.'[2] Was he right in attributing such high significance to a changed attitude to the Bible? That is the subject before us.

By way of a preliminary comment let me say that my object in taking up this subject is practical rather than controversial. Last year the Presbyterian church building where I was brought up finally closed its doors. It is a fine building, opened by George

[1] An address at the Crieff Fellowship Conference, January 9, 2013.
[2] *English History 1914-1945* (Oxford: Clarendon Press, 1965), p. 168.

Adam Smith in 1900, and able to seat perhaps a thousand people. The closure came not because there was anything wrong with the building; it was one of the thousands of churches which fell victim to what Taylor called the 'great happening' of a century ago. There were simply not enough Bible preachers or Bible hearers to keep it open. We are living today in the aftermath of a changed view of Christianity which has come into the British Isles. To ask the question why this happened is to ask something of very practical significance. In the first instance it has to be a subject for grief and humiliation rather than for argument and controversy.

Change in three stages

The changed attitude to Scripture occurred in approximately three successive stages. The first might be said to cover the twenty years, 1860–1880. This was the introductory period when a new approach to Scripture began to take hold in Britain. It did not happen without controversy, but for the most part the teaching produced no general alarm. Of course, the ideas were not new in 1860. A student who came back from a German university in 1852 told his minister, 'You do not *read* the Bible. You turn over the leaves, but you do not analyse, and compare book with book, and part with part. In Germany we study the Bible as we do any other book, and we find in it what you have not discovered; we find in it literary blemishes, historical inaccuracies and contradictions.'[1]

This young man was a forerunner of the many who would come back from mid-nineteenth-century Germany convinced that they had been at the fountain head of Christian scholarship.

[1] R. Watts, *The New Apologetic and its Claims to Confessional Authority* (Edinburgh: Maclaren, 1879), p. 3.

The opinion spread that for ability in understanding Scripture, the German universities were leading the world. They proposed a new starting point: instead of the submission to its text which had been traditional, it should be read as 'any other book'. This approach needed a new name. Those who favoured it called it 'the new apologetic'. By others it was designated 'the higher criticism'.

The opening years of the 1860s saw the first collision between clergy in the Church of England on this issue. It started with seven Anglican clergy who authored the volume *Essays and Reviews*, a book which favoured the argument that Scripture should be interpreted like 'any other book'. This was followed up by the writing of Bishop Colenso who believed that the Old Testament could not possibly be taken as accurate history. From the other side, Dean Burgon replied, 'The Bible is none other than *the Word of God*: not some part of it, more, some part less; but all alike, the utterance of Him who sits upon the Throne;—absolute, faultless, unerring, supreme!'[1]

Scotland was only a few years behind this beginning of controversy. It was occasioned by a published sermon of the young Marcus Dods (1834–1909), *Revelation and Inspiration,* in 1877. Dods, a minister of the Free Church of Scotland, was a former pupil of A. B. Davidson. Davidson had become Professor of Hebrew and Old Testament at New College, Edinburgh in 1863, and, while reticent himself to challenge traditional belief in Scripture in public, he cautiously gave higher criticism to his students, the brightest of whom—including Marcus Dods—he encouraged to study further in Germany.

[1] J. W. Burgon, *Inspiration and Interpretation, Seven Sermons before the University of Oxford in 1860–61,* p. 89.

Dods' published sermon was answered in a review by Hugh Martin and, in 'deference to his brethren', Dods stopped its sale.[1] More open controversy was postponed, but in this first period a quiet infiltration of the new attitude to Scripture continued and slowly spread in Presbyterian and other denominations. Had there been a real trial of strength at that date, the exponents of the new would have failed; as it was, Bishop Colenso was dismissed from his post, and was Davidson's pupil, Professor Robertson Smith of the Free Church of Scotland from his chair in Aberdeen. 'Of course', writes Willis B. Glover, 'in 1860 the verbal inspiration of the Bible was still the majority belief, and even the mildest criticism was almost sure to run afoul of an inerrant Bible'.[2]

The second stage in this history began around 1880 and ran towards the dawn of the twentieth century. These years saw the new teaching becoming widely accepted. Even so, the acceptance was more in theological colleges than in congregations. Professors who had themselves studied in Germany were now enthusing an admiring generation of young men. Robertson Smith was the last to be silenced in the Free Church; his teaching continued to be promoted by others of marked ability, including Marcus Dods

---

[1] Hugh Martin responded more fully in *Letters to Marcus Dods* (London: Nisbet, 1877), and, with a wider bearing, *The Westminster Doctrine of the Inspiration of Scripture* of the same date and publisher.

[2] Willis B. Glover, *Evangelical Nonconformists and Higher Criticism in the Nineteenth Century* (London: Independent Press, 1954), p. 49. Evidence for this statement is not lacking. A. S. Farrar in the Bampton Lectures of 1862 wrote, 'Protestantism reposes implicitly on what it believes to be the divine authority of the books of Holy Scripture.' *A Critical History of Free Thought in reference to the Christian Religion* (London: John Murray, 1862), p. viii. 'With a few exceptions', he writes, 'the belief in the full inspiration was held from the earliest times' (p. 668).

and George Adam Smith. In the course of their professorships in Edinburgh and Glasgow respectively, both Dods and G. A. Smith would be tried for heresy, and both would be cleared.[1] Such was the general change taking place that their view of Scripture was now being presented as the only view worthy of a real scholar. The years 1880–1900 saw higher criticism firmly established in theological education. Even in 1881, with some exaggeration, Prof. C. A. Briggs could assert:

> The great majority of professional Biblical scholars in the various Universities and Theological Halls of the world, embracing those of the greatest learning, industry and piety, demand a revision of traditional theories of the Bible.[2]

A third period in this history was to follow, and it is in the aftermath of this period that we still live. Now higher criticism was no longer limited to theological halls or academic books; it was diffused almost without challenge, far and wide throughout Protestant denominations. What had once been the common belief of Christians came now to be seen as the creed of a remnant, named 'obscurantists' or 'fundamentalists'.

In the Baptist Union in England higher criticism had been the cause of the major controversy in 1887–88, during which Spurgeon resigned his membership. But in 1925 all was peaceful when Dr T. R. Glover became President of the Baptist Union. It was one of Spurgeon's biographers, W. Y. Fullerton, who described Glover as

---

[1] I have written more fully on 'The Tragedy of the Free Church of Scotland' in *A Scottish Christian Heritage* (Edinburgh: The Banner of Truth Trust, 2006), pp. 369-96.

[2] C. A. Briggs, 'Critical Theories of the Sacred Scriptures in Relation to their Inspiration', *Presbyterian Review* (New York: Randolph, 1881), p. 557.

'a prophet whom God has sent us'. The heresy of yesterday had become the new orthodoxy. 'Verbal inspiration', said Glover, 'is a monstrous belief. Religion must depend upon something more verifiable than . . . detached sayings attributed to Jesus.' Glover's greater knowledge of Scripture included such things as his statement that where the editor of the Book of Kings 'was bored he got over the ground at an alarming rate.' Or again, 'Luke clearly did not like Mark's style.'

In articles in *The Times* in 1932, surveying current theological education, Glover wrote triumphantly, 'Today, if you want a real old obscurantist college, you have to found a new one.'[1] In the course of those articles, Glover referred to the parallel scene in Methodism and spoke of the debt owed to the Methodist theologian, Arthur S. Peake. In 1919 Peake had produced an influential 1,000-page commentary on the Bible. But, while seeming to encourage the study of the Scriptures, at the same time he gave his readers reason to doubt whether any such study was worthwhile. He warned: 'In reading the Old Testament we are not dealing with history at all, in the modern sense of the term. . . . Myth and legend are noted as though they were actual occurrences.' At times, he believed, Scripture is only a record of 'the imperfect morality ascribed to Yahweh'. When he came to the New Testament Peake gave his readers the same uncertainties. 'We are still far from having any proof that we have the *ipsissima verba* of Jesus, or any guarantee that the events of His life are related with absolute accuracy in the Gospels.' Again, 'We must be prepared to allow for the growth of a quasi-legendary element.' No wonder Paul's

[1] E. J. Poole-Connor, *Evangelicalism in England* (London: FIEC, 1951), pp. 249-51.

words are credited with little authority. The apostle's teaching on the resurrection of the body in 1 Corinthians 15 is described by Peake as 'one of his most daring pieces of speculation'.[1]

At a Methodist Conference in Australia, in the 1920s, Peake's commentary was adopted as the textbook for all probationers preparing for the ministry. A minority protested against the adoption including the veteran minister, Dr W. H. Fitchett of Melbourne, who declared that the decision would mean that in the future the churches would have 'a tattered Bible and a mutilated Christ'. Far from listening to Fitchett, the Assembly wrote to tell Dr Peake of its decision, which it described as 'a vote for truth and thousands will thank God'.[2]

The same thing was happening in the Presbyterian Church of Ireland. In 1925, W. J. Grier, a student in preparation for the ministry of that church, came back from two years at Princeton Theological Seminary. Before him was a final year of study at the Irish Presbyterian College. Here a very different teaching prevailed in its lecture halls. He heard Professor J. E. Davey teach the class that Paul did not claim anywhere that Christ pre-existed as God before he came into this world. Grier challenged him with the words of Philippians 2:6-7, 'who, being in the form of God . . . took upon him the form of a servant, and was made in the likeness of men'. At the beginning of his next lecture, Davey admitted that Paul did teach this, only to add immediately, 'My faith is not in Paul'. At the same time another professor in the college was teaching six reasons for not believing in the inerrancy of the Scriptures.

[1] *Ibid.*, pp. 265-6.

[2] Iain H. Murray, *Australian Christian Life* (Edinburgh: The Banner of Truth Trust, 1998), p. 337.

When objections to this line of teaching became vocal they led a reluctant General Assembly to examine charges against Professor Davey in 1928. The professor openly acknowledged statements used against him. He had referred to 'discrepancies' in the Scriptures. Indeed, he wrote, 'without hesitation I should say there are literally hundreds of discrepancies or direct contradictions in Old and New Testaments'. 'We are not', he said, 'as Christians committed to an intellectual infallibility of either Christ or the Bible.' The outcome was that the Assembly approved Davey by a vote of 707 to 82, and he was subsequently made Principal of the College. The guilty party was not the professor but the few who had brought the case against him, as they were duly admonished.[1]

In the Church of England things were little different. In 1912 H. Hensley Henson, Dean of Durham and later to be its Bishop, wrote on 'The Intellectual Failure of Puritanism'. He believed that without fear of contradiction he could say: 'The attitude of unquestioning and literal acceptance which determined the Puritan's handling of the Bible, and made it for him a sufficient directory of conduct in all situations, has passed forever.'[2]

Prominent among those who had promoted this thinking in the Church of England were the clergy of the Modern Churchmen's Union, an organization formed in 1898 for the 'advancement of Liberal Religious Thought'. In January 1930, after Bishop Barnes, a leader in this Union, had given an address on the Progress of Modernism, he received a letter of admonition from

[1] W. J. Grier, *The Origin and Witness of the Irish Evangelical Church* (Belfast: Evangelical Book Shop, 1945), pp. 38-41. Prof. Davey, at his trial, assured the General Assembly that he had received 'the second blessing' at the Keswick Convention.

[2] In his three-volume autobiography, *Retrospect of an Unimportant Life* (1942–50) Henson scorned Christians of evangelical belief .

William Temple, the Archbishop of Canterbury. But what disturbed Temple was not the unbelief of Barnes, it was his thinking that the Modern Churchmen's Union was still needed. He found it 'objectionable' that Barnes seemed to limit to Modernists,

> a great deal which is held by all educated Christians, it implies that those who do not wish to be so described do not hold these views . . . You say 'the story of the Virgin Birth cannot be used to prove the divinity of Christ'. Armitage Robinson said the same in his popular little book *The Study of the Gospels* in about 1900. No one was surprised. He was saying what was already accepted among educated people. You say that ten years ago a religious teacher who accepted evolution was still suspect. Suspect to whom? Not to any ecclesiastical authority. When my Father announced and defended his acceptance of evolution in his Brough lectures in 1884 it provoked no serious criticism.

Temple went on to comment on how 'education' had similarly changed belief in Adam and Eve and in the atonement, and this brought him to the point of his letter:

> Personally I regret the existence of a special organization of Modernists. Modernism, as you yourself describe it, is an intellectual movement leavening the whole Church, and quite indispensable to its progress or even survival. But to separate out the people specially concerned with it weakens their leavening capacity, and stiffens others in resistance.[1]

In his period the same process of change in belief was happening in the United States.[2]

[1] F. A. Iremonger, *William Temple, Life & Letters* (London: OUP, 1948), pp. 490-2. His father, Frederick, was Archbishop of Canterbury 1896–1902.

[2] For a striking illustration see R. B. Hobbs, *How Big is your God? The Spiritual*

Explaining the change

A. J. P. Taylor was right to speak of the significance of the change in Britain as being 'as great a happening as any in English history since the conversion of the Anglo Saxons to Christianity'. This ought to lead us to the question, *Why did Christians in Britain ever give entrance to such a reversal of belief on Scripture?* The question is so fundamental that it is very surprising it is so little considered. How is it to be explained? Could it be that Christians agreed that the trustworthiness of Scripture was not necessary for Christianity to survive? Did they think that faith could stand without the Bible? Were they simply ready to give unbelief free entrance in the denominations?

I do not believe that an explanation along those lines is possible. We have to look elsewhere. When German higher criticism was first heard of in Britain it was widely identified with unbelief, and for that reason it made slow headway. But by the 1880s the perspective was changing. Now the exponents of the higher criticism came to be identified as men of evangelical belief. Marcus Dods called himself 'an evangelist'. The students of Arthur S. Peake, it is said, saw their teacher as 'a unique combination of the higher critic and the evangelist'. The friends of T. R. Glover, spoke of 'the depth of his evangelical experience'. William Robertson

---

Legacy of Sam Patterson (RTSFCA: French Camp, Mississippi, 2010). In 1963 Mr Patterson wrote to the presidents of the four leading theological seminaries of the Presbyterian Church in the United States. In response to the question, 'Do we need an infallible Bible?' the answer was we do not need one because we do not have one. The above volume follows the result of Patterson's enquiry (pp. 180-196 *etc.*). The effect of the teaching of these seminaries had been: '1. Vacant and spiritually hopeless, small churches. 2. Pastored but hopeless, stunted churches. 3. Millions of homes with no Sunday School or church relationship.'

Nicoll, influential editor of the *British Weekly,* used his pen both to favour higher criticism and to extol the gifts of friends who were its exponents. He thought Dr Denney deserved to be described as 'the most accomplished divine and teacher in the English Church'.[1] Marcus Dods was 'the most Christlike man I have ever known'.[2] What he called 'the brilliant literary and theological renaissance of the Free Church' was due, he affirmed, 'to Drummond and to a few of his contemporaries'.[3]

The compatibility of the new teaching with evangelical faith was not to be questioned. Far from being a case of unbelief, it was argued that a more critical view of Scripture would actually promote the gospel. The change was not a defeat but an advance. It was claimed that greater success for Christianity would surely follow an acceptance of 'the new apologetic'.

What they emphasised was that the future of the faith lay, not in the words of a book, but in the living Christ. Scripture is a guide, helpful as a sign post to a traveller on the road, but the presence of a living Christ is better than any sign post. Which is preferable, it was asked, to be dependent on 'the letter' of the Bible, or to have the personal guidance of Christ? So, they promised, to move on from the traditional view of the inerrancy of Scripture would not be to belittle Christ; on the contrary, it would give him greater honour. R. W. Dale was only repeating the words of many when he said, 'The Church of Christ is not under the

[1] *Letters of Denney,* p. xxvii.

[2] W. R. Nicoll, *Princes of the Church* (London: Hodder and Stoughton, 1921), p. 234.

[3] *Ibid.,* p. 96. Henry Drummond (1851–97), Scottish evangelist, writer and lecturer.—See also p. 54.

bondage of the "letter"; it has the freedom of the Spirit.' Dale's book, *The Living Christ and the Four Gospels* (1890) spoke of this advance and assured preachers: 'There is now no authority to come between *us*—to come between the *congregations* to which you and I have to minister, and Him who is the very truth of God.'

In Scotland none of the leaders of higher criticism repudiated the evangelical belief. James Denney was saying the same thing as Dale when he contrasted the joy and liberty of the gospel with what he called 'the unlearned piety' which 'swears by verbal, even by literal inspiration, and takes up to mere documents an attitude which in principle is fatal to Christianity'.[1]

Such was the way in which the case against an inerrant Bible was presented. Assurance was given to the churches that to embrace the change would not be detrimental to the evangel, rather it would combine 'new light' with sound evangelical experience.

Unless the persuasiveness of this line of argument is recognised, it is impossible to understand why so many evangelicals gave the movement their support. Alexander Whyte is an instance of an evangelical who believed that the gospel and the 'new apologetic' could go forward together. His biographer tells us that when the orthodoxy of Robertson Smith's teaching was being debated at the General Assembly in Edinburgh, it was Whyte's manse which 'became a kind of committee room for the Robertson Smith party'. When Smith was first acquitted by the General Assembly of 1880, that same night a thanksgiving service was

---

[1] James Denney, *The Second Epistle to the Corinthians* (London: Hodder and Stoughton, n.d.), p. 126. Denney told the General Assembly, 'for verbal inspiration he cared not one straw'. P. C. Simpson, *Life of Principal Rainy* (London: Hodder and Stoughton, n.d.), vol. 2, p. 115.

held in the home of Whyte's bride-to-be, Janie Barbour, between 1 and 2 a.m. The next year, when the decision went the other way, and Smith's post was terminated, Whyte took part in a meeting to protest the action of the Assembly.[1]

To say this, however, is by no means to give the whole explanation as to why it was thought that a changed view of Scripture would be beneficial to the faith. The key lies in the historical context of the late nineteenth century. It was an age of intellectual turmoil in which the credibility of Christianity and of the Bible was being challenged on several fronts at once—belief in evolution, the supposed discoveries of geology, the 'findings' of German higher criticism, all combined to question inerrant Scripture. 'Modern thought' and the churches were drawing far apart. In what amounted to a panic, teachers within the church concluded that concessions would have to be made. They feared that to stand by the whole text of Scripture would put the churches at a serious disadvantage among thinking people.

But instead of being a threat, could it be that higher criticism offered a solution? Supposing that the distinction made between authentic and unreliable Scripture is irrefutable, why not accept the distinction and let Christians confine themselves to a defence of the authentic? Evangelical truth—the essential *substance* of the Faith—could then be upheld without any need to defend *all* that is in the Bible. Surely to assert the great centralities would be enough, and by taking this course the contemporary challenge to Christian faith would be blunted.

Such was the motivation of many who believed in 'the new apologetic'. They presented their different view of Scripture in a

[1] G. F. Barbour, *Life of Alexander Whyte,* pp. 212, 220-1, 228.

positive light. It was not a retrograde step but a wise move with the times. Traditional belief in inerrancy belonged to yesterday; change was necessary for the credibility of the church in the modern world. Such was the message heard from scores of voices.

One of the most popular of those voices was that of Henry Drummond, hero-worshipped in Scotland and beyond, both as a scientist and an evangelical. In *The Life of Henry Drummond,* by Professor George Adam Smith, we are told, somewhat apologetically, that Drummond shared in the D. L. Moody missions in Glasgow in 1873–5. But by the time of his death in 1897, Drummond had, in Smith's words, 'travelled from the positions of the older orthodoxy', and from Moody's 'narrow and unscriptural theory of inspiration':

> And upon the new positions to which he was led he has evidently found a basis for his faith more stable than ever the old was imagined to be—richer mines of Christian experience, better vantage grounds for preaching the Gospel of Christ, and loftier summits with infinitely wider prospects of the power of God, and of the destiny of man.[1]

Among the advocates of this thinking, opinions differed over whether or not the Bible teaches that its text claims to be inerrant. There were those who believed it made no such claim, and they sometimes tried to argue that Christianity was never committed to a belief in inerrancy. On the other hand, the majority among the teachers of higher criticism conceded that Scripture does claim to be inerrant, but they regarded it as belonging with

---

[1] G. A. Smith, *Life of Henry Drummond* (Hodder and Stoughton, 1910), 243-4. See also p. 92. This was the eleventh edition of this title, 'completing 35,000 copies'. 'Verbal inspiration', he believed, 'prevents thinking' (p. 371 n.).

the unreliable parts of the text. So, although Jesus attributed the opening books of Scripture to Moses, it had to be recognised, they said, that the belief of Jesus was conditioned by the thinking of his time. In John 10:34 Jesus quoted part of a verse in Psalm 82 as authority for a particular truth, but in doing so he extended that same authority to all Scripture, affirming, 'the Scripture cannot be broken' (*John* 10:35). In the face of such words, the new apologetic could only say that all statements attributed to Christ are not necessarily reliable.

To support this thinking a new phrase became fashionable, and it was built into the revised Formulas of the Presbyterian churches. No longer was it to be agreed that Scripture is the word of God; the older affirmation was changed to, 'The Word of God *contained* in Scripture.' But who is to tell *where* it is contained? And who is to recognise how much of God's word does Scripture contain—a verse here, perhaps, or a chapter there? Who is to judge what is trustworthy and what is not?

Evangelicals were slow to recognise the gulf which such questions were bound to open up. It was all very well to say that 'the substance' of Scripture is sound, and that its central message can still be upheld, but who is to formulate that message if there is no certainty about individual statements, even of those of Christ himself? It was a short step between doubting what Christ says on the trustworthiness of Scripture to doubting everything he said.

No real answer was given to this problem. Some looked for a solution by making a difference between spiritual truths and alleged history: 'We believe the spiritual truths, but we do not believe all that is presented as historical facts.' But it is plain to see in Scripture that the meaning of spiritual truths is bound up with facts. The ruin of the human race is inseparable from the historic fall of Adam—'by one man sin entered into the world' (*Rom.* 5:12); the virgin birth belongs with the sinlessness of the Son of God; the reliability of Christ's promises and the authenticity of his miracles stand together; the bodily resurrection of those who die in Jesus is tied to the history of his rising from the grave.

Others made a different distinction. They said they believed in 'revelation' but not in the infallibility of the human record of that revelation. The revelation is trustworthy—could we know it clearly—but Scripture is the human response to revelation and is only the writing of fallible men. But, again, such a solution leads nowhere. If we do not know that the words of Scripture are trustworthy, how can we be sure of any revelation separable from those words?

I have already mentioned how the advocates of limited truth in the Bible sought to escape from this problem. They professed that it need not be a problem because Christ is able to interpret the truth to us in personal experience; therefore we can rest, not on the external authority of old documents but on his living testimony to us. The authority of Christ can be the substitute for the authority of Scripture. But the assurance this offers quickly broke down under closer examination. As B. B. Warfield argued powerfully against Marcus Dods, if we do not receive the Christ who is made known to us in Scripture—the Christ who said of Scripture, 'It cannot be broken'—then the alternative is *another* Christ, or, indeed, *many* Christs, all modified according to personal opinion. Dr Dods, Warfield wrote, believed that he preserved enough of Christ for Christians to be content,

But what about the Christ that Wernel gives us? Or Wrede? or Oscar Holtzmann? or Auguste Sabatier? or Reville? or Brandt? or Harnack? Which Christ of the fallible Scriptures shall we be ultimately forced to put up with? Will He become to us at length only a vague figure who lived in Galilee nineteen centuries ago?[1]

Long before this criticism, Dods' own father, Marcus Dods (1786–1838), minister of Belford in Northumberland, wrote against the unbelief into which his son was to lapse and gave this warning:

We can frame theories and devise rules by which we may determine when the volume which comes to us as '*all* given by inspiration of God', really speaks the word of God, and when it exhibits only the wisdom of man. And is it when we read in this way, that the word of God will become to us the fountain of life, and the well of salvation? Alas! No.[2]

The 'church' replacing the Bible

The advocates of the new did not lack the intelligence to see that, if the basis for belief is only subjective personal experience, then there can be no sure faith, only endless diversity of opinion. One escape was left, and it was seized on by the denominations. Not the individual but the church must decide the truth. Thus, the Presbyterian Church of Ireland, in its revised Rule of Faith, spoke of 'the Word of God which is contained in the Scriptures of the

---

[1] B. B. Warfield, *Critical Reviews* (New York: OUP, 1932), p. 125, reviewing Dods' *The Bible, its Origin and Nature* (1905).

[2] Comment on Romans 10:17, entry for Jan. 13 in, *The Christian Souvenir, or Reflections for Every Day in the Year, Selected from approved authors* (Edinburgh: Oliphant, 1829).

Old and New Testament'. The awkward question which the word 'contained' poses was met by this addition, 'In the Church resides the right to interpret and explain her standards under the guidance of the Holy Spirit.'[1] The Formula to be signed by ministers and elders in the Church of Scotland settled on the same solution. It acknowledges, 'The Word of God, contained in the Scriptures of the Old and New Testaments to be the supreme rule of faith and life,' and 'as its subordinate standard the Westminster Confession of Faith, recognizing liberty of opinion on such points of doctrine as do not enter into the substance of the Faith and claiming the right, in dependence on the promised guidance of the Holy Spirit, to formulate, interpret, or modify its subordinate standards: always in agreement with the Word of God and the fundamental doctrines of the Christian faith contained in the Confession, of which agreement the Church itself shall be the sole judge.'

The last words are the clinching, determinative statement, *'of which agreement the Church itself shall be the sole judge'*. The words have the effect they were intended to have: the General Assembly is the final authority in deciding what the faith is. Does that provision secure that a body of truth will be handed down from one generation to another? It does not. It was General Assemblies which eulogized George Adam Smith and Marcus Dods for the very opinions for which Robertson Smith had earlier been removed from his post by another Assembly. So within a few years the composition and beliefs of General Assemblies may undergo remarkable changes. If a General Assembly is made up of believing men, then its opinion may be a safe guide to the churches, although that opinion can never be the rule of faith

[1] Grier, *Origin and Witness*, pp. 24-5.

for the Christian's faith. But where the composition of a General Assembly is of a different kind, the consequences of this claim are disastrous. As two writers, reflecting on the changed Formula, wrote in 1910: 'The Standards of the Church are at the mercy of all the winds of doctrine that may blow; there is no supreme and definite rule by which even the vagaries of theological speculation may be tried.'[1] Henceforth the Christian faith would be whatever the General Assembly said it would be. This was an assumption of authority which God never gave to any church. As the Westminster Confession says: 'All synods or councils since the apostles' times, whether general or particular, may err, and many have erred; therefore they are not to be made the rule of faith or practice, but to be used as an help in both'(xxxi:4).[2]

The hope that the church could advance with a fallible Bible was fatally flawed. Willis Glover summarises the position in the words: 'Evangelical Christians felt the need for some theory of inspiration that would recognize the fact of errors in the Bible and yet guarantee its objective authority as a final court of appeal in doctrinal matters. It was a false hope embodying a fundamental contradiction, but it had immense influence in the development of religious opinion in England.'[3]

---

[1] A. Stewart and J. Kennedy Cameron, *The Free Church of Scotland 1843–1910* (Edinburgh & Glasgow, 1910), p. 123. The prospect of such changes in belief did not worry everyone. W. R. Mathews, who became Dean of St Paul's, said: 'We are probably the first generation of Christians to whom the serious possibility has presented itself that the Christian religion itself may be only a transitory episode in the spiritual pilgrimage of Mankind.' E. J. Poole-Connor, *The Apostasy of English Nonconformity* (London: Thynne, 1933), p. 19.

[2] See also the 39 Articles, xix, 'As the Church of Jerusalem, Alexandria, and Antioch, have erred; so also the Church of Rome hath erred.'

[3] *Evangelical Nonconformists and Higher Criticism*, p. 89.

The reality: man's word broken

It is an indictment of human folly that those who were so enthusiastic about the brighter future contained in their changed view of Scripture did not foresee what was coming. The promises and assurances they gave were unfulfilled. Instead, desolation was to come to both church and nation. Yet there were some higher critics who foresaw the future, and one of them was Marcus Dods himself. From the 1860s he led the way in opposition to the verbal inspiration of Scripture. His teaching and ministry majored on the 'optimistic acceptance of criticism'. But in 1907 he was to give this opinion of the position to which the supposed advance in knowledge had led them:

> It is amazing on the one hand to see how little Christians understand Christ; and on the other hand to see how instinctively men of all religions adore what is good, and how often they seek to possess it. It's a strange, unintelligible world, and the one fixed point on which hope can rest is that God is Father of all.

In a private letter Dods made this chilling forecast on Scotland's future: 'The churches won't know themselves fifty years hence. It is to be hoped some little rag of faith may be left when all's done.'[1]

Perhaps William Robertson Nicoll before his death had come to see the great mistake which he had promoted. Keith Ives, his most recent biographer, has written: 'What he and his generation handed on was, in spite of their best intentions, a flawed and weakened church, which seems to have lost its way.'[2] Certainly the optimism seems to have faded in Nicoll. He wrote to a friend

[1] *Later Letters of Marcus Dods* (London: Hodder and Stoughton, 1911), p. 67.

[2] K. A. Ives, *Voice of Nonconformity, William Robertson Nicoll and the British Weekly* (Cambridge: Lutterworth Press, 2011), p. 245.

in 1900:

> I am deeply concerned every day about the love of pleasure and the want of seriousness among the younger people of our richer classes. Things come under my notice as a minister which would give any man cause for serious thought. It appears to me that if society is to be saved, and if the church in especial is to do her proper work, there must be a return to the great Puritan idea of separation from the world. So far as I know, except for a few extreme people—very few now—there is no difference between the church and the world.[1]

Eta Linnemann, was a teacher of higher criticism in the university system of West Germany. She wrote in 1990:

> In its own eyes, historical-critical theology wants to lend assistance to the proclamation of the gospel through an interpretation of the Bible that is scientifically reliable and objective. There is, however, a monstrous contradiction between what it says it wants to do, on the one hand, and what it actually does, on the other. It does not further the proclamation of the gospel—in fact, it actually prevents it.[2]

Dr Linnemann discovered this by coming to a saving knowledge of Christ. Liberal theology had removed the foundation of Scripture and, 'If the foundations be destroyed what can the righteous do?' (*Psa.* 11:3)

---

[1] T. H. Darlow, *William Robertson Nicoll, Life and Letters* (London: Hodder and Stoughton, 1925), pp. 165-6.

[2] Eta Linnemann, *Historical Criticism of the Bible, Reflections of a Bultmann-ian turned evangelical,* trans. R. W. Yarbrough (Grand Rapids: Baker, 1991), p. 89. Linnemann came to see that the theology she had formerly taught was 'a sign of God's judgment' (p. 18).

Lessons

1. History shows the need to watch against the misuse of words.
The misuse may be accidental, or it may be deliberate. Words can come to us in disguise so that we embrace what we did not intend to embrace. A confusion in vocabulary was certainly to be found in the debate over the trustworthiness of Scripture, and it clouded the issue. In particular, men began to speak of the 'infallibility of Scripture' but meaning something less that the reliability all Scripture and its verbal inspiration. But the authority which Scripture claims for itself is an authority expressed in words: it is *writing* which is 'breathed out of God' (*2 Tim.* 3:16). David *spoke* 'by the Spirit' Jesus affirmed, as did all the Prophets (*2 Pet.* 1:21). Paul affirms, 'we speak, not in the words which man's wisdom teaches, but which the Holy Spirit teaches' (*1 Cor.* 2:13). Christ gave us *the words* which the Father had given him (*John* 17:8). 'Heaven and earth shall pass away: but my words shall not pass away' (*Luke* 21:33)—not one small particle of them, not 'one jot or tittle' (*Matt.* 5:18). True infallibility means, and can only mean, verbal inerrancy.

On the difference between Spurgeon and others over this issue, Willis Glover makes this valuable observation:

> Spurgeon saw very clearly that inspiration in its traditional sense meant inerrancy. To talk about the divine inspiration of an erring record was to use the term in an entirely different sense, and this simply bred confusion. But other evangelicals preferred to be confused. They answered in all sincerity that nobody believed in inspiration more strongly than they. Then they imputed their own confusion to Spurgeon and accused him of being vague.[1]

---

[1] *Evangelical Nonconformists and Higher Criticism,* p. 167.

At a later date Dr J. I. Packer has written of how he encountered the same problem. He refers to evangelicals who have sometimes lacked wisdom or grace in teaching inerrancy, and who thereby give needless offence. Not wanting to be linked with them, he says, he declined to use the term 'inerrant Scripture'. In the course of time, however, he came to see that he was wrong:

> Once I too avoided the word *inerrancy* as much as I could . . . But I find that nowadays I need the word. Verbal currency, as we know, can be devalued. Any word can have some of its meaning rubbed off, and this has happened to all my preferred terms for stating my belief about the Bible. I hear people declare Scripture *inspired* and in the next breath say that it misleads from time to time. I hear them call it *infallible and authoritative*, and find they mean only that its impact on us will keep us in God's grace, not that it is all true.[1]

Packer believes that evangelicals became scared of speaking of inerrancy. But the real problem which the world has with Scripture cannot be met by changing words. It is what the word means that is the real cause of offence, and we are only engaging in double talk if we propose other words for inerrancy which, in truth, mean the same thing. Better, Packer says, to be honest and face the offence.

Another example of how words were used in a different sense from their original use has to do with the phrase in the Westminster Shorter Catechism, 'the word of God, which is contained in the scriptures of the Old and New Testaments'. The word 'contained', left on its own, is ambiguous, and it was deliberately left

[1] *Truth & Power: The Place of Scripture in the Christian Life* (Guildford, Surrey: Eagle 1996), pp. 46-7.

like that in the revised Formulas of the Presbyterian Churches. But a look at the Westminster documents shows unmistakably that the authors did not mean the words 'contained in' to refer to *a part* of Scripture to be distinguished from *other parts*. Any such interpretation they expressly contradicted: 'The holy scriptures of the Old and New Testaments are the word of God.' 'It pleased the Lord . . . for the better preserving and propagating of the truth, and for the sure establishment and comfort of the Church against the corruption of the flesh, and the malice of Satan, and of the world, to commit the same wholly unto writing.' The word of God and the written word are identical.[1]

2. *The inerrancy of Scripture is not a truth which stands alone.* Where it is not accepted there are consequences for the Christian faith as a whole.

In the mercy of God, individuals may be true believers in Christ, although, for lack of fuller understanding, they may hesitate over the inerrancy of all Scripture. People do not need to have a true doctrine of Scripture before they can trust in Christ. Commitment to the inerrancy of Scripture is not the prerequisite for saving faith. New life may come to sinners before they have ever seen a Bible.

Nevertheless, authentic Christianity will not be long preserved where Scripture is not recognised as the watershed between truth and error. On one side of the watershed is submission to all that God has spoken; on the other side is the human wish to decide what is trustworthy and what is not. On the right side lies certainty and finality; on the wrong side, doubt and apostasy. Once the division which Scripture constitutes between the wisdom of God

[1] Larger Catechism, Q.3, and Confession of Faith, i:1.

and the wisdom of the world is unrecognised, there can be no consistent Christianity. All manner of doubts may enter. Cease to treat all Scripture as the word of God, and the route leads downwards to Dods' 'little rag of faith'.

Once man is given leave to decide what he will trust in Scripture and what he will not, there need be no uncertainty about what will be laid aside. It will be the truths most uncongenial to fallen human nature. Original sin will go; the Ten Commandments will go; the wrath of God on sin will go; the strait gate and the narrow way leading to life will go. Once it is thought that we are at liberty to modify, or discard Scripture, it will not be Christianity that is left.

Countless now empty church buildings bear witness to this fact. The mainline denominations provide tragic proof. They did not set out to arrive at the position which has been reached. It began when they chose the wrong side of the watershed.

The same lesson is seen in the lives of individuals. Dr James Denney, as a young minister, gave the Church in Scotland the prospect of his being an eminent evangelical leader. His early books, such as his *The Second Epistle to the Corinthians* (1894), had a warm evangelical note, but from the outset the inerrancy of Scripture was not part of his thinking and from its absence a downward trend followed. He found himself in a process of accommodations with what he called 'the modern mind'. In 1908, his friend William Robertson Nicoll wrote to him of his concern that Denney's latest book, *Jesus and the Gospel*, contained no 'clear assertion that Jesus Christ is God'. Denney replied to Nicoll that he 'would not think it a New Testament thought, that God is

Father, Son, and Holy Ghost'.[1] Dismayed, Nicoll commented to Professor H. R. Mackintosh that Denney's thinking would allow Arians and Unitarians into the ministry of the church, and he added, 'There is a singular vein of scepticism in him, for all his apparent orthodoxy. For instance, he does not believe in the existence of the devil and of evil spirits. Nor does he believe in the Second Advent.' Denney's last book was *The Christian Doctrine of Reconciliation*, published posthumously in 1917. It was reviewed by Professor C. Wistar Hodge of Princeton and the review makes sober reading. Hodge starts by recalling Denney's earlier teaching, and he goes on to show the change which had taken place. In his final work Denney,

> cannot allow that Christ's death was in any sense penal; nor that Christ's work fully satisfied Divine justice; nor that our guilt is imputed to Christ; nor His righteousness to us. All these ideas Dr Denney explicitly rejects. . . . He cannot allow that Christ acted as the sinner's Substitute in the fullest sense of that term.[2]

The root problem, Hodge noted, was that the objective authority of the New Testament did not control Denney's thinking. His view of the atonement had become, 'an interpretation of Christian experience', and not 'a formulation of the New Testament teaching'. Denney thought that 'experience', as well as exegesis, is

---

[1] T. H. Darlow, *William Robertson Nicoll, Life and Letters*, p. 364. What Denney wrote to Nicoll on the subject are in *Letters of Principal James Denney to W. Robertson Nicoll* (London: Hodder and Stoughton, 1920), pp. 120-6. They do not contain the quotation I have given, perhaps edited out by Nicoll who certainly understood his friend's thought.

[2] 'Dr Denney and the Doctrine of the Atonement', *Princeton Theological Review*, October 1918, pp. 626.

necessary to arrive at Christian truth. He wrote: 'Our whole conception of revelation and of Scripture has changed. No doctrine is for us *merely* a question of exegesis'[1] (emphasis is in the original). This position, Hodge noted, led Dr Denney, 'unconsciously perhaps, to modify the New Testament teaching where he does not like it'.[2] What Denney's position meant was that Christians cannot any more build doctrines simply on the text of Scripture.[3]

Denney's case confirms the general principle. Once the verbal inspiration of Scripture is set aside the way is open for all manner of conjectures. A consensus of agreement on biblical truth has been proved impossible where there is no agreement on verbal inerrancy. In 1950 the leaders of the Student Christian Movement asked for a private discussion with leaders of the Inter-Varsity Fellowship (now UCCF), in the hope that they could reach an agreement on belief. There was only one stumblingblock, they said, namely the IVF's doctrine of Scripture. If only that could be removed there could be unity. But the upshot of those discussions was that the difference over Scripture affected the SCM's thinking on virtually every major Christian doctrine. Ultimately they differed on the doctrine of God himself.

Evangelicals have sometimes failed to recognise the significance of the watershed. There have been responses to liberal beliefs on a whole series of issues—women bishops and homo-

[1] *Letters of Principal James Denney,* p. 126.

[2] *Princeton Theological Review,* October 1918, p. 638..

[3] Yet this is precisely what Christ did. He established his deity by an appeal to a sentence in one verse (*Matt.* 22:43 and *Psa.* 110:1), and the doctrine of the resurrection of the dead from the one word, 'I am the God of Abraham' (*Matt.* 22:32)—Abraham still lived before God and that made the resurrection of Abraham's body certain.

sexual marriage being the latest—without addressing the fact that unity is impossible where there is no agreement on the authority of Scripture. On this point, Packer also has a striking comment in which he also criticises himself. With reference to the ongoing controversy between evangelicals and liberals in North America, he writes that in the stand for Christian fundamentals,

> biblical inerrancy was from the first made the touchstone more directly and explicitly than was ever the case in the parallel debates in Britain. This, I now think (I did not always think so), argues for clearer-sightedness in the New World, for without inerrancy the structure of biblical authority as evangelicals conceive it collapses.[1]

3. *The place of Scripture cannot be rightly understood unless it is seen in the context of the superhuman and the demonic.* It is when he was tempted of the devil that we read our Lord saying so emphatically, 'It is written. . . . Again it is written. . . . Be gone, Satan! for it is written . . .'(*Matt.* 4:4-10). It is when Paul is teaching Christians that, 'we wrestle not against flesh and blood, but against principalities, against powers, against the rulers of the darkness of this world', that he enforces the necessity of our taking 'the sword of the Spirit which is the word of God' (*Eph.* 6:12, 17). In contrast to

---

[1] *Truth & Power,* p. 91. The effect of Christians not upholding the inerrancy of Scripture is particularly seen in the British universities where evangelicals may gain teaching positions if they adhere to the ground rules imposed by the rationalistic tradition. 'Evangelicals working in this milieu have followed the tradition and argued for a conservative position on exclusively rational grounds. They have been pushed into this policy by the desire to defend biblical teaching in the only way that others will accept.' Oliver Barclay, *Evangelicalism in Britain 1935–1995* (Leicester: IVP, 1997), p. 129. 'Christianity has always been a matter of divine revelation rather than what can be argued for by human wisdom. No university now in Britain would claim that for them "the fear of the Lord is the beginning of wisdom."' (p. 131)

this, the literature from Germany which promoted higher criticism commonly showed total neglect of the superhuman. It was the same with the liberal theology which followed. Nothing was said of another order of fallen beings active among the human race and with an intelligence surpassing that of men. The fact was not so much argued against as totally ignored. Modern thought rested on the assumption that, given the right education, and the right intellectual ability, we can settle the truth for ourselves.

This is a plain denial of the teaching of the New Testament of the condition of man in sin. No man by nature has any saving knowledge of God. No man by nature even has the capacity for that knowledge. Worse, no one even *wants* that knowledge. An antagonism to God, an antipathy to the truth of God, is universal in fallen human nature. 'The mind of the flesh is enmity against God' (*Rom.* 8:7). We 'love darkness' rather than light. 'The natural man receiveth not the things of the Spirit of God: for they are foolishness unto him: neither can he know them, for they are spiritually discerned' (*1 Cor.* 2:14).

Here is the fundamental reason for the different attitude of the Christian and the non-Christian towards the Bible. One person says, 'O how I love thy law, it is my meditation all the day. The words of thy mouth are better unto me than thousands of gold and silver. My heart stands in awe at thy word.' Or with William Cowper,

> A glory gilds the sacred page,
> Majestic like the sun.

But anyone not 'born of the Spirit' sees nothing amazing in Scripture. The warnings and the promises do not touch him. He has the same nature as King Jehoiakim who took a knife to the writing of Jeremiah and threw the pieces into the fire (*Jer.* 36:23). The explanation is, 'the god of this world has blinded the minds of them which believe not' (2 *Cor.* 4:4). Christ teaches this with the utmost clarity. The world's hatred of the Christian is due to the Christian's connection with God's word: 'I have given them thy word; and the world has hated them, because they are not of the world' (*John* 17:14). In the Revelation of John believers are described as those 'slain for the word of God' (*Rev.* 6:9) and as those 'which keep the sayings of this book' (*Rev.* 6:9; 22:9).

Christ teaches in the most unmistakable way that the unbeliever's attitude to Scripture derives from Satan; it comes from fallen man's relationship to him: 'Why do ye not understand my speech? Even because ye cannot hear my word. Ye are of your father the devil . . . Because I tell you the truth, ye believe me not . . . he that is of God, heareth God's words: ye therefore hear them not, because ye are not of God' (*John* 8:43-7).

The late-nineteenth-century compromise over Scripture in the church took no account of Satanic influence. It missed the truth that the wisdom of God and the wisdom of this world are antithetical. There is no possibility of accommodating the one to the other. 'The Spirit of truth', Jesus said, is the Spirit 'whom the world cannot receive' (*John* 14:17). The quest to win the approval of 'the modern mind' was in itself a denial of Scripture. Until renewed by the Spirit of God the mind of the natural man will not receive the truth. He is captive to the one whom Jesus describes as a 'murderer from the beginning' and a 'liar'. Satan uses superhuman power and wisdom to keep men from the one book given to make them 'wise unto salvation'. The terrible truth is that the devil wants men cursed, not blessed, and he knows the way that curse comes. It is by teaching men to trust in themselves, for Scripture says, 'Cursed be the man that trusteth in man . . . he shall be like the heath in the desert, and shall not see when good cometh; but shall inhabit the parched places in the wilderness' (*Jer.* 17:5, 6).

Of course, the devil acts with human agency. He works in and through men. If he can, he will do this even through believers (*Matt.* 16:23). He works especially through human pride;[1] he aims to give us high views of ourselves and never to suspect that there is anything wrong with our minds. He knows how we like to be flattered. Flattery and the praise of men were prominent in the whole higher critical movement. Professing Christians fell over themselves in praising one another for their wonderful scholarly achievements. The whole foundation of higher criticism and liberalism was faith in man. Its leaders were lauded and eulogised. Honours were showered upon them. Some of them were knighted. Their characters and abilities were considered beyond reproach. George Adam Smith, one of the foremost of the Bible critics, was given the position of Chancellor at Aberdeen University. It is not for us to adjudicate on the characters of these men, but we can say that the ethos in which they lived had no place for such commands of Christ as, 'Call no man Teacher', or 'Beware of men.' A group of great men they undoubtedly were, but they led a multitude, who admired and trusted them, into catastrophe.[2] If their

---

[1] On this see *The Nature and Causes of Apostasy from the Gospel,* in *Works of John Owen,* ed. W. H. Goold, vol. 7 (Edinburgh: The Banner of Truth Trust, 2009), pp. 123-34.

[2] It would be hard to account for Nicoll's support of the higher-critical leaders

teaching had been judged by Scripture there would have been a different outcome. 'Put not your trust in princes, nor in the son of man, in whom there is no help. His breath goeth forth, he returneth to his earth; in that very day his thoughts perish' (*Psa.* 146:3, 4).

4. *The Bible is not in our hands, to treat as we think or please.* It belongs to God. He owns it. He fulfils its promises. He brings to pass its blessings and its judgments. We are not its judge. We are frail, mortal men, to whom God says, 'Your fathers where are they? But my words and my statutes did they not take hold of your fathers?' (*Zech.* 1:5, 6). God is eternal, and so is his word: 'All flesh is as grass, and all the glory of man as the flower of grass. But the word of the Lord endureth for ever' (*1 Pet.* 1:24, 25).

Faith in Scripture is also in God's hands to give. If it depended on us no one would believe the Bible. It needs the power of the Creator to break into our darkness. As Calvin writes, we do not come to faith in Scripture by disputing and reasoning, but by the Spirit who gives his own irresistible testimony to the truth: 'The testimony of the Spirit is more excellent than all reason. For as God alone is a fit witness of himself in his word, so also the word will not find acceptance in men's hearts before it is sealed by the

without taking this into account. In 1887, as editor of the *British Weekly*, he wrote: 'Nor do we know of a single statement in the Old Testament that has been clearly disproved.' Yet at that date he was already, as Willis Glover wrote, making his other publication, the *Expositor*, 'the primary vehicle of higher criticism in England' (*Evangelical Nonconformists and Higher Criticism*, p. 154). At the earlier date he had simply accepted what his friends had told him, 'that the position of "believing critics" gave confidence to the preacher in his use of the Old Testament. The truth was that his [subsequent] published sermons and articles show that he had all but abandoned the Old Testament. For, far from "believing criticism" giving him confidence, he personally hardly ever preached from the Old Testament, and if he did, he did not expound but used the text in a poetic or mystical way.' Keith A. Ives, *Voices of Nonconformity, William Robertson Nicoll and the British Weekly*, p. 188.

inward testimony of the Spirit.' 'And man's understanding, thus beamed by the light of the Holy Spirit, then at last begins to taste those things which belong to the kingdom of God, having formerly been quite foolish and dull in tasting them.' Paul 'denies that man himself initiates faith . . . faith does not depend upon men's wisdom, but is founded on the might of the Spirit (*1 Cor.* 2:4, 5)'.[1]

Once a person experiences this, the whole of life becomes oriented and attracted to Scripture. The Christian has entered a school where God is his teacher. So he prays: '*Teach me*, O Lord, the way of thy statutes . . . *Give me* understanding, and I shall keep thy law . . . *Make me* to go in the path of thy commandments . . . *Incline my heart* unto thy testimonies' (*Psa.* 119:33-36).

The supernatural nature of Scripture has immense bearing on the position of the unconverted. God identifies himself with Scripture, and to turn from Scripture is to turn from God. This is the explanation of the history of Israel. To be given the 'oracles of God' was their highest privilege. 'He sheweth his word unto Jacob, his statutes and his judgments unto Israel. He hath not dealt so with any nation' (*Psa.* 147:19, 20). God's charge against them was: 'I have written to him the great things of my law, but they were counted as a strange thing' (*Hos.* 8:12). Instead of trembling at God's word, they so ignored it that it was lost in the time of King Josiah. Only after its rediscovery did Josiah tear his clothes in grief and confess, 'Great is the wrath of the Lord that is kindled against us, because our fathers have not hearkened unto the words of this book' (*2 Kings* 22:13). All who despise the word

---

[1] *Institutes of the Christian Religion,* trans. F. W. Battles (Philadelphia: Westminster), I:vii:4; III:ii:34-35.

will awake to find it against them. Those who will not honour it shall lose it: 'Behold the days come, saith the Lord God, that I will send a famine in the land, not a famine of bread, nor a thirst for water, but of hearing the words of the Lord' (*Amos* 8:12).

The state of our land today is a clear fulfilment of Scripture. As Israel, we have 'sown the wind, and we reap the whirlwind'. But the judgment is not all now. Worse is ahead. To the unbelieving hearer of his words, Jesus says, 'The word that I have spoken, the same shall judge him in the last day' (*John* 12:48). To dishonour his word is to dishonour Christ himself, and, 'whosoever shall fall on this stone shall be broken: but on whomsoever it shall fall, it will grind him to powder'(*Matt.* 21:44). In that day the kings of the earth, and the great men, and the rich men, will say to the mountains and rocks, 'Fall on us, and hide us from the face of him that sitteth on the throne, and from the wrath of the Lamb' (*Rev.* 6:16).[1] 'Whosoever shall be ashamed of me and of my words in this adulterous and sinful generation; of him also shall the Son of man be ashamed, when he cometh in the glory of his Father with the holy angels' (*Mark* 8:38).

5. *The fact that the Bible is in God's hands is the believer's great encouragement.*

The nineteenth-century idea that the church had to make concessions to the 'modern mind' to retain influence was unbelief.

---

[1] Prof. A. B. Bruce was contemptuous of such reasoning and told his students: 'The anxious maintenance of the dogma of inerrancy tends to foster a legal attitude of mind in our whole way of thinking about God. We are apt to think of God as concerned for His dignity and reputation as an Author.' Quoted by M. MacAskill, *The New Theology in the Free Church* (Edinburgh: Hunter, 1892). Bruce was Professor of Apologetics in the Free Church College, Glasgow. Bruce's words are reminiscent of the serpent's—'Ye shall not surely die' (*Gen.* 3:4).

The Bible needs no human approval or endorsement to make it effective. 'For it is written, I will destroy the wisdom of the wise, and will bring to nothing the understanding of the prudent' (*1 Cor.* 1:19).

The message we have to preach is that there is no hope in human nature. Is that depressing? It is to all who do not know that God reigns in grace and power. He brings 'the blind by a way that they knew not'. He 'convicts the world of sin, and of righteousness, and of judgment'. As he first gave light by his command at the creation, he commands today the light which must shine in dark hearts.

No revival in the church and the world has ever come through human plans and arrangements. Light and faith have sprung up in times utterly contrary to the gospel, times when whole populations have been immersed in materialism with no concern for spiritual things. It was like that in Britain in the sixteenth century before the Reformation. Then men and women with no previous interest in, or hunger for Scripture, suddenly found an insatiable hunger for the word of God. They began to live for it, to suffer for it, die for it. Something parallel is happening in China today where one hundred and twenty million Bibles have been published since the end of the cultural revolution. This always happens in the same way. It is God owning his own word, and the Holy Spirit anointing men to preach Christ. Whenever God gives men 'full of faith and the Holy Spirit' wonderful things are going to follow. Christ came to send fire on the earth, and it is that fire which is committed into the hands of preachers: 'Is not my word like as a fire? saith the Lord; and like a hammer that breaks the rock in pieces?' (*Jer.* 23:29).

We have looked at sad history—a professing church in Britain defeated by the world. All kinds of remedies have been promoted but the situation grows worse. The first need is to understand how this happened. It was not by flesh and blood. The attack came from the author of lies and unbelief. God is able to renew our faith. He can take away our fear of man and our half-hearted attachment to his word. The supreme need for the ministry today is to give first place to 'the sword of the Spirit'. Then the churches will see another fulfilment of the promise: 'My Spirit which is in you, and the words that I have put in your mouth, and the mouths of your offspring, shall never fail' (*Isa.* 59:21).

Can we expect to see a revival? Long ago John Owen answered this very question, and his words still stand true today. It will come, he said,

> When God shall revive and increase a holy, humble, zealous, self-denying, powerful ministry, by the more plentiful effusion of the Spirit from above; then, and not until then, may we hope to see the pristine glory and beauty of our religion restored unto its primitive state and condition.[1]

Let our resolution therefore be the same as John Wesley's:

> I am a creature of a day, passing through life as an arrow through the air. I want to know one thing: the way to heaven; how to land safe on that happy shore. God himself has condescended to teach that way; for this very end he came down from heaven. He has written it down in a book! O give me that book! At any price, Give me the Book of God! I have it: here is knowledge enough for me. Let me be, 'a man of one book'.[2]

[1] Owen, *Works*, vol. 7, p. 195.
[2] Preface to *Sermons on Several Occasions* (London: 1825), p. vii.

Note 1

Scripture and the Holy Spirit

In the age of rising unbelief in Scotland there was a remnant who understood the gravity of the situation. One of them was the Rev. Hugh Martin, who wrote to a friend on 19 November, 1879:

My Dear Friend,—Do you understand the state of things in our poor church? I do not. What I am afraid for is the doctrine of the Trinity. Of course, shallow folks (and they are too numerous) would laugh at my saying so. But although I cannot enter on it here, let me tell you that a church's hold on the doctrine of the Trinity is affected by her hold of the doctrine of the inspiration of Scripture. For it is in virtue of a truly inspired Word—His own Word—that the Holy Spirit acts as a person. It is degradation to the Third Person of the Godhead to suppose that He would speak by the word or words of any person less than Himself. He does not speak at all as a person by any word less than His own Word, or the Word of the Son, or the Word of the Father, all which are one. To suppose the Spirit coming by a new and fresh revelation is of course Quakerism, but in His coming by a previously writ-ten inspired Word, He acts as a person. As a person He speaks, enlightens, convinces, persuades, and renews. Deal falsely with personality here, then the Holy Spirit does not combine with the Second Person, but falls back upon an impersonal Deity—a Thing. You have merely what is implied in 'God is a Spirit', but Word is gone, Father is gone, Sonship is gone, Messiahship is gone, Mediatorial position is gone, infernal robbery has been committed, and the mists of darkness have settled down upon the church! Yea, we are not a church at all, for we are robbed of a divine revelation, of a divine record. The privileges and position of a church are given 'chiefly because unto them were committed the oracles of God'. Alas! that so many who ought to be teachers deal as falsely and irreverently with the oracles of God as a cat playing with her kitten, or a kitten with a cork.

I am sorely afraid that there will be a great decline in our church. If you meet any after I am gone who do courageously stand for all revealed truth, give them my compliments, and tell them to be strong and of a good courage. Let them not yield to the current sentimental Christianity that would convert men's faith in a living, glorious, inexhaustible, infallible Word into empty-headed, empty-hearted speculations no better than Chinese puzzles or acted charades. God will avenge such trifling. 'The Scripture cannot be broken', is the testimony of Him who is Himself the eternal Word. And will He suffer it to go unpunished if the divine truth—which He has in infinite condescension been pleased to make known to men by means of an infallibly inspired record—be broken up into bits and shreds, into fragments and fancies? And if the 'Lord will not hold them guiltless who takes his name in vain', He will not, assuredly, hold that church guiltless which tolerates any profaning or abusing of that Word by which He hath made Himself known.[1]

[1] 'Letters of the Late Rev. Hugh Martin, D.D', *Free Presbyterian Magazine,* May, 1897.

Note 2

Fundamental Christian Truth and the Essence of Evangelical Faith

Adam S. Storey, *A Critical History of Free Thought in reference to the Christian Religion,* Bampton Lectures 1862.

The standard of truth here adopted, as the point of view of criticism, is the teaching of Scripture as expressed in the dogmatic teaching of the creeds of the church; or, if it will facilitate clearness to be more definite, three great truths may be specified, which present themselves to the writer's mind as the very foundation of the Christian religion: (1) the doctrine of the reality of the vicarious atonement of Christ provided by the passion of our blessed Lord; (2) the supernatural and miraculous character of the religious revelation in the book of God; and (3) the direct operation of the Holy Ghost in converting and communing with the human soul. Lacking the first of these, Christianity appears to him to be a religion without a system of redemption; lacking the second, a doctrine without authority; lacking the third, a system of ethics without spiritual power.

3

APOSTASY[1]

'Apostasy' is an ugly word that speaks of an ugly subject. Our older divines, knowing no one English word to stand for abandoning and deserting God, brought the original Greek, *apostasia,* into our language. I take it up conscious that in handling it, there are at least two dangers:

1. The danger of being too dogmatic in the interpretation of our own times. Our understanding of the providence of God is very limited. The words of Ecclesiastes 8:17 teach that God's doings cannot be fathomed even by the wise: 'I saw all the work of God, that man cannot find out the work that is done under the sun.' There are many situations that we cannot understand. Even when the great Reformation of the sixteenth century had begun, Martin Luther could write to his friend John von Staupitz in 1522, 'The Lord knows the end of it. The matter is beyond our power of comprehension and understanding.'[2]

On one aspect of the subject of apostasy it is particularly important to recognize our ignorance: there is more than one

---

[1] An address delivered in several places.
[2] *Luther's Works,* vol. 49 (Philadelphia: Fortress Press, 1972), p. 12.

form of apostasy. When a professing Christian abandons the faith, we cannot tell *at the time* whether the behaviour is temporary or permanent. Archbishop Thomas Cranmer, under the pressure of persecution, denied his evangelical and Protestant faith. At that point no one knew that he would yet ascend a pulpit to denounce his recantation, and then at the stake hold out his hand to the fire with the words, 'Forasmuch as my hand offended, in writing contrary to my heart, my hand shall be first punished therefore.' There is a temporary apostasy, followed by recovery, and an apostasy which is total and irrecoverable. The latter is the apostasy spoken of in Hebrews 6:6 where we read of those for whom there is no possibility of them being 'renewed again unto repentance'. Once these people professed repentance; to all appearances they became real Christians, 'they tasted the word of God'—as those in our Lord's parable, 'when they hear, receive the word with joy' (*Luke* 8:13)—but slowly it all disappeared and in the end they are utterly indifferent or opposed to spiritual things. When backsliding begins no one can tell where it will end. It is well that we cannot tell the difference between these two classes of people, for it means we are to despair of none.

2. *The danger of spreading discouragement.* We do not need an emphasis on the dark and gloomy side of things. We are to 'rejoice in the Lord always'. We have all met Christians or seen religious papers that seem to specialise in being pessimistic. Their habit is to be reporters of bad news. The outcome of this practice is inevitably depressing. In addition it is also dangerous, for it leads others to associate words of warning with 'cranks' to whom there is no need to listen.

I accept these are real dangers. But nevertheless I take up this subject because I believe it needs attention, and I begin with reasons why it is important.

1. *The prominence given to the danger of apostasy in Scripture*

If we neglect this subject, or treat it lightly, our thinking is not in accord with the word of God. Apostasy is falling away from light and privileges that were once known and professed. It is a major theme in the Old Testament account of the people of God. We see it in the children of Israel in the wilderness, in the ten tribes of the northern kingdom, in individuals such as King Saul and King Solomon. It is prominent in the teaching of our Lord. He tells us that by no means all who seem to belong to him will continue: 'If a man abide not in me, he is cast forth as a branch, and is withered; and men gather them and they are cast into the fire' (*John* 15:6). One of his own disciples belonged to that category, and Jesus has warned us to expect the same in the future. When the disciples ask him the time of his second coming, instead of telling them, he warns that they need to expect days of apostasy. 'As it was in the days of Noah, so shall it be also in the days of the Son of man' (*Luke* 17:26). 'Many false prophets shall arise and shall deceive many. And because iniquity shall abound, the love of many shall wax cold' (*Matt.* 24:11, 12). And these warnings were proved relevant in the churches of the apostolic age. There was not a New Testament church that did not need warning. The churches of Rome, Corinth, Thessalonica, Ephesus and Colosse are all warned. Sometimes whole letters major on the theme. The disciples in Galatia were so enthusiastic for Christ and his servant that they would have been willing to give their very eyes to Paul. But in his letter to them the apostle stands in doubt of them: 'I am afraid of you, lest I have bestowed upon you labour in vain' (*Gal.* 4:11). The letter of Jude was written expressly to seek to arrest apostasy. Paul tells the church at Thessalonica that instead of uninterrupted progress for the gospel, there would be a future declension into a counterfeit Christianity and urges, 'Let no man deceive you by any means' (2 *Thess.* 2:3).[1] Again, Paul, writing to Timothy, says, 'The Spirit expressly says that in the later seasons some will depart from'—apostatize from—'the faith' (*1 Tim.* 4:1). 'Expressly', that is, clearly, definitely. The Spirit speaks of periods when 'seducing spirits' will achieve success. Men will depart from the faith.

But the fullest treatment of apostasy is in the Epistle to the Hebrews. Thousands of Jews professed faith and became disciples of Christ; many of them suffered much for Christ's sake; but now the question had arisen, how many of them were going to continue to be committed to Christ? Hence the alarming words of the letter: 'We are made partakers of Christ, if we hold the beginning of our confidence stedfast unto the end' (3:14). 'Let us therefore fear, lest, a promise being left us of entering into his rest, any of you should seem to come short of it' (4:1). 'Cast not away your confidence' (10:35). 'Looking diligently lest any man fail of the grace of God' (12:15).

This is surely enough to remind us that this is no incidental subject that scarcely warrants our attention.

---

[1] On this point, Thomas Manton notes that teaching about Antichrist is 'very necessary to be preached and known . . . if it were profitable for them that were to go out of the body long before Antichrist was revealed, certainly it is more profitable for others that live at the time these things are in being.' *Works of Thomas Manton,* vol. 3 (Nisbet: London, 1871), p. 48.

2. In twenty-first-century Britain we are living in an age of apostasy.

I will not seek to prove this by repeating facts with which we are all familiar. It would be more profitable to consider the characteristics of times of apostasy as given in Scripture and to compare what we know with those descriptions.

(1.) Self-satisfaction and self-confidence are marks of times of apostasy. Speaking generally, we hear little said today on the subject of apostasy. When I look at some of our contemporary theological dictionaries I find no entry on the subject. Few write on the subject. In the late nineteenth century such preachers as J. C. Ryle and C. H. Spurgeon spoke very plainly of apostasy, but little is heard about it today. How can this be explained apart from an unwarranted confidence? Simon Peter was about to have his greatest fall when he was most confident: 'I will lay down my life for thy sake' (*John* 13:37). The church at Laodicea said, 'I am rich, and increased with goods, and have need of nothing', and did not know how near they were to being spewed out of Christ's mouth. When Dr Lloyd-Jones was asked, 'Do you think revival near?' He replied, 'No, I do not. We are far too healthy.' When churches ignore the danger of apostasy it is often a sign that the condition has already begun.

(2.) Widespread worldliness in the church is a characteristic of apostasy. This is what we find in Genesis 6: 'the sons of God married the daughters of men'. There is surely no reason to be puzzled about the meaning of that verse. The line of Seth and Enoch, the believing 'seed of the woman' (*Gen.* 3:15), ceased to see any importance in not intermarrying with the offspring of Cain. The distinctiveness of church and world was lost as both

merged together, and it was this that brought on the Flood. 'The Flood came, not because the Cainite race had become corrupt, but because the race of the righteous had fallen into sensual pleasures.'[1] We tend to think of apostasy only in terms of departure from orthodox belief, but apostasy is also described in Scripture in terms of character and behaviour. This is what we find in 2 Peter. The Apostle Peter speaks of those who 'once escaped the defilements of the world through the knowledge of our Lord and Saviour Jesus Christ'. But they were like Balaam; the world took hold of them again, they 'turned back from the holy commandment delivered to them'. They began to think that the holiness of the gospel was too narrow for them. Peter says they were advocates of liberty and yet were 'slaves of corruption'. How is one to account for the contemporary silence on the Ten Commandments, the decline of Sunday evening worship, the film reviews in evangelical papers which assume that Christians enjoy the diet of contemporary entertainment, apart from worldliness in the churches? Do films that treat it as normal that men and women have 'eyes full of adultery' fall within the apostolic command, 'whatever is pure, whatever is lovely, whatever is of good report, if there is any excellence and if anything worthy of praise, dwell on these things' (*Phil.* 4:8).

(*3.) No concern for the evidence of history* is another common mark of apostasy. Forgetting the past was a regular sign of declension in the Old Testament. The people of God were called to hand down a heritage; but instead 'They forsook the Lord God of their fathers, which brought them out of the land of Egypt' (*Judg.* 2:12). This same attitude arose in Britain at the end of the nineteenth

---

[1] Luther, *Works*, vol. 2 (St Louis: Concordia, 1960), p. 12.

century. The cry was: 'We are the enlightened generation. We are advanced beyond the simplicities of our fathers. They were traditionalists and did not have our knowledge. How can the past teach us?' So the historic Articles, Confessions, Catechisms, even the Ten Commandments, largely disappeared from the churches. This was an attitude quite contrary to Scripture. How often the word of God appeals to lessons highly relevant for present conduct in all ages! Jesus said, 'As it was in the days of Noah so shall it be also in the days of the Son of man' (*Luke* 17:26). He tells us to 'Remember Lot's wife.' Repeatedly the New Testament holds up the example of the children of Israel in their journey to Canaan as an example of permanent relevance. Six hundred thousand left Egypt. They saw the mighty works of God, when the Red Sea parted and Sinai shook; 'But with many of them God was not well pleased: for they were overthrown in the wilderness' (*1 Cor.* 10:5). 'Therefore, as the Holy Spirit says, Today, if you hear his voice, do not harden your hearts as the children of Israel did in the wilderness' (*Heb.* 3:7, 8).

History commands very little interest in Christian circles today. Few people in the churches know the past or ask how we got to into the present spiritual conditions. When such ignorance exists opinions of all kinds will flourish. One popular illusion in evangelical circles is that evangelicalism in the period between 1900 and the Second World War is not worth studying. It is said that the evangelicals of those days were only 'pietists'. 'They were not scholars. They lacked the ability to address their culture. They were too prone to live in ghettos.' I believe that is a gross caricature. Men such as Canon Christopher of St Aldate's, Griffith Thomas of Wycliffe Hall, E. A. Knox of Manchester, Stuart

Holden of St Paul's, Portman Square, were representative evangelicals of that era and far removed from such a description. I fear a main reason why such men came to be forgotten was that their testimony did not coincide with that of their successors. For one thing, they were all Protestants. In 1927–28, when it seemed the Revised Prayer Book might get the approval of Parliament, almost 1,000 evangelical clergy meeting at Church House took a solemn pledge that 'they would leave the Church of England if the Prayer Book measure was passed'. They asserted that the new Book 'introduces into our Formularies doctrines contrary to God's Word and that we will not consent to them at any price'. Archbishop Marcus Loane, who has written on this period, called this successful protest, 'The high-water mark of Evangelical strength and achievement between the two World Wars.'[1] His assessment represents a different view from the one popular today.

The leaders of a former age sought to be faithful when many British churches were sliding into apostasy. They saw the danger and spoke out. H. E. Fox, Prebendary of St Paul's and Secretary of the Church Missionary Society, warned:

> Who is not conscious that reverence for sacred things, regard for the day of rest, respect for the sanctities of family life, or even for decency in public amusements, are much less than they were a generation ago? Such consequences come, not from the increase of faith in God and His Word, but from the decrease.... A Church infected with rationalism is crippled in its mission to the world. It loses its evangelistic spirit, and if it still sends forth missionaries,

[1] M. L. Loane, *These Happy Warriors* (Blackwood, S. Australia: New Creation, 1988), p. 4. See also *Makers of our Heritage*, pp. 135-6.

they will too often be men who have only a broken evangel for non-Christian people.[1]

(4.) When interest in the churches begins to centre round the visual and the sensual it is commonly a sign of impending apostasy. By 'sensual' I mean that which appeals to the senses of man (sight, smell, hearing), as opposed to 'spirit', that is, the capacity that belongs to those born of the Spirit of God. Hence the antithesis, 'sensual, having not the Spirit' (*Jude* 19). 'Sensual' is also translated 'natural' or 'worldly'; the meaning is the same. It does not take regeneration to give the sensual or the aesthetic a religious appeal to the natural man or woman.

In the Old Testament the people of God were in measure taught by their senses as God imposed the form of worship. As a check against any misuse of that means of teaching, no additions or subtractions from it were allowed. But with the finished work of Christ, and the coming of the Holy Spirit, a momentous change took place. The church was raised to the higher privilege of worship in 'spirit and truth' (*John* 4:24). She belongs to the 'Jerusalem which is above' (*Gal.* 4:26). In the words of John Owen, 'the naked simplicity of gospel institutions' was established in the place of 'the old, glorious worship of the temple'; Levite choirs, incense, vestments, *etc.,*—all were gone. Yet not gone permanently, for as church and world came gradually together in the rise of the Papacy, worship that appealed to the senses came back. Presuming on Old Testament practice, what the gospel had ended in the apostolic age was restored, and the difference made by Pentecost

---

[1] *Rationalism or the Gospel?* pp. 21-2.

disappeared.[1] Instead there developed a form of worship in Roman Catholicism which made impressions at the natural level and did not need the Holy Spirit.

In the words of Richard Bennett, long a Roman priest, 'The ritual, symbolical richness of the sacramental life of the Church, to a great extent, meets the human need for transcendence.'[2] It does no more than that. The observation of W. H. Griffith Thomas, writing on 'Spiritual Worship', is true: 'It is the universal experience of Christian people that the more the senses are attracted, fascinated, and occupied, the less room there is for the action of the soul. The teaching of Christian History points very clearly to the fact that simplicity of outward ceremonial has been usually accompanied by the reality of the inward spirit of worship.'[3]

This is where the neglect of church history and Scripture has serious consequences for many contemporary evangelical churches. In the 1960s, at a time when the churches were losing their hold on young people, it was believed that a new way of

---

[1] 'Dislike of the purity and simplicity of the gospel worship is that which was the rise of, and gave increase or progress unto the whole Roman apostasy. Men do not like the plain institutions of Christ, but are pleased with the meretricious Roman paint, wherewith so great a part of the world hath been beguiled and infatuated.' Owen, *Works*, vol. 21, pp. 114-5, also identified as his *Exposition of Hebrews*, vol. 4 (Edinburgh: The Banner of Truth Trust, 1991). Likewise he argues that what was being addressed in the Epistle to the Hebrews was the temptation of professing Christians to regret the loss of the visual glory of Judaism. Owen's *Nature and Causes of Apostasy from the Gospel*, in *Works*, vol. 7 is unsurpassed as a treatment of the subject.

[2] R. Bennett, *Catholicism: East of Eden* (Edinburgh: The Banner of Truth Trust, 2010), p. 44.

[3] W. H. Griffith Thomas, *The Catholic Faith, A Manual of Instruction for Members of the Church of England* (London: Church Book Room Press, 1955) p. 147.

renewing contact with them was to be learned from the contemporary culture. Music appeals to all, and why not make use of the new style of music and accompaniments which had become so popular? After all, music has to be neutral, so why not make it an ally?[4] Some put it more strongly. James Ryle 'prophesied' that 'God is getting ready to anoint Christian musicians with the same anointing that was given to the Beatles', and he attributed to God the words, 'I had a purpose, and the purpose was to usher in the charismatic renewal with music revival around the world.'[5]

Few warning voices were to be heard. Martyn Lloyd-Jones was almost alone in the 1960s in England when he warned against 'the increasing tendency at the present time' to use music to produce emotion; the justification being that music can make people happy, and when people feel happy they will find Christianity more acceptable. When an older generation sometimes expressed misgivings at the change this thinking had brought into public worship, they were told not to put their wishes before those of the outsiders whom the church needed to win. Few saw the danger pinpointed by Lloyd-Jones: the impression of music on natural feelings was being confused with spiritual truth: 'Because it [music] is performed in connection with a religious service or by Christians, people imagine and persuade themselves that they are feeling the truth. But they are not. This feeling has no direct connection with what they have believed.'[6]

[4] That music is 'neutral' is by no means always true. 'Since music should help the reception of the Word of God, it should be weighty, dignified, majestic and modest; fitting attitudes for sinful creatures in the presence of God' (Calvin).

[5] Quoted by John MacArthur, *Charismatic Chaos* (Grand Rapids; Zondervan, 1992), p. 72.

[6] D. M. Lloyd-Jones, *Living Water: Studies in John 4* (Wheaton: Crossway,

With this new departure came a flood of musical innovations into evangelical churches worldwide. The instruments of the old temple worship, as well as others, were restored, and with 'music teams' and 'music directors', public worship has undergone a transformation.

It would be a mistake to say the change has come simply from the initiative of evangelicals. The Roman Catholic Church is no less involved, and in her case the new thinking was not new at all. It was under the Papacy, in the later Middle Ages, that the church first commonly took up the use of instrumental music. At the time of the Reformation, Erasmus complained of the Roman churches: 'We have brought into our churches a certain operose and theatrical music . . . as I think was ever heard in any of the Grecian or Roman theatres. The church rings with the noise of trumpets, pipes and dulcimers; and human voices strive to bear their part with them . . . Men run to church as to a theatre, to have their ears tickled.'[1]

2009), p. 365. He added: 'If you start clapping your hands or stamping your feet or moving them in a rhythmatic manner, you are the whole time dealing with this realm of the emotions. And there is a great deal of that today. Some even deliberately employ psychological methods—different coloured lights, for instance, to prey upon the emotions' (p. 366).

[1] Quoted by John L. Girardeau, *Instrumental Music in the Public Worship of the Church* (Richmond, VA; 1888), p. 162. R. L. Dabney, reviewing and commending Girardeau's book, made the same point at Dr Lloyd-Jones: 'Blinded men are ever prone to imagine that they have religious feelings, because they have sensuous, animal feelings, in accidental juxtaposition with religious places, words, or sights. This is the pernicious mistake which has sealed up millions of self-deceived souls in hell.' *Dr Girardeau's Instrumental Music in Public Worship, A Review* (Richmond, VA: 1889), p. 8.

The Reformers rejected the paraphernalia of musical accompaniments, not because they did not appreciate the place of congregational song in the worship of God, but, on the contrary, because they wanted its restoration to New Testament simplicity. In the words of Calvin: 'In gospel times we must not have recourse to these, unless we wish to destroy the evangelical perfection, and to obscure the meridian light which we enjoy in Christ.'[1] Far from having any right to claim the support of Scripture for what Rome had introduced, he further says: 'Now that Christ has appeared, and the church has reached full age, it were only to bury the light of the gospel, should we introduce the shadows of a departed dispensation.'[2]

The Church of Rome, in her apostasy, has long exhibited the full outworking of the danger which evangelicalism is now ignoring. But sometimes protest came from an unexpected quarter to break the silence. Richard Bennett, after finishing his education at the Angelicum University of Rome, served as a priest in Trinidad. In all his years there, he writes, Protestant Christians from overseas sometimes came to services,

> saw our sacred oils, holy water, medals, statues, vestments, rituals, and never said a word! The marvellous style, symbolism, music, and artistic taste of the Roman Church were all very captivating. Incense not only smells pungent, but to the mind it spells mystery. One day, a woman challenged me (the only Christian ever to challenge me in all my twenty-two years as a priest), 'You Roman

[1] On 1 Samuel 18:1-9.

[2] On Psalm 92:3, quoted by C. H. Spurgeon, whose church also used no instrumental music, *The Treasury of David,* vol. 4 (London; Marshall, Morgan, & Scott, 1950), p. 123. Many Protestant churches have used *one* instrument instead of a precentor to set the tune; this is very different from the instrumental accompaniment that is now promoted.

Catholics have a form of godliness, but you deny its power.' Those words bothered me for some time because the lights, banners, folk music, guitars and drums were dear to me. Clearly I was unable to apply the Scripture to my life where it mattered most.[1]

The change in public worship in evangelical churches is not the harmless thing it is thought to be. 'So long as there is good preaching', it is said, 'we need not be overly concerned.' We ought to be concerned! An appetite is being fed which in the past has led to the very abandonment of the gospel. When satisfying the 'natural' becomes acceptable in churches, the spiritual will not long remain. As the long-time Catholic and later Protestant martyr, Hugh Latimer, warned, 'When candles go up, preaching comes down.'

That music has great prominence in modern society is not in doubt. Nor is it the first time that such attention has been given to music in periods of decadence. Horatius Bonar noted:

In connection with the 'decline and fall' of the Roman Empire, a singular fact has been recorded.—When the arts were declining,—poetry, sculpture, painting, deteriorating,—religion and patriotism decaying,—music was cultivated to an extraordinary extent. Old Roman died music-mad.[2]

Accommodating the churches to contemporary culture may increase numbers (for a time); it has never led to a spiritual awakening. Unless there is a God-given change, we will see in evangelicalism a developing apostasy.

---

[1] *Catholicism: East of Eden,* pp. 9-10.
[2] H. Bonar, *Our Ministry* (Edinburgh: MacNiven 1883), p. 74.

(5.) An absence of zeal for the truth is a characteristic of apostasy. The Bible speaks of it being a time of disaster when 'truth is fallen in the street . . . yea, truth fails; and he that departs from evil makes himself a prey' (*Isa.* 59:14, 15). In 2 Chronicles 15 we read, 'Now for a long season Israel had been without the true God, and without a teaching priest, and without law.'

Definite commitment to truth and opposition to error have always been unpopular but in times of declension it is most notably so. When Anglo-Catholic belief was gaining influence at Oxford, Canon Christopher was reproached for making it a subject of controversy, and for chairing a Protestant meeting where Dr Pusey was criticised. E H. Liddon wrote to Christopher, chastising him; to which Christopher replied:

> If not in this life, assuredly dear Dr Liddon in another, it will be made clear to you that to speak earnestly and valiantly for Divine truth, even if in doing so the speaker has to blame to the face and by name one revered for his years and position, is entirely compatible with Christian love and the bond of peace.[1]

On the same theme Christopher wrote again:

> In love to God and to our fellow men around us we should endeavour to correct with Bible Truth corruptions of the Gospel. Every clergyman of the Church of England at his ordination was asked by the Bishop this question: 'Will you be ready with all faithful diligence, to banish and drive away all erroneous & strange doctrines contrary to God's Word?' . . . Controversy is simply the correction of religious error with God's truth . . . Without controversy the

[1] J. S. Reynolds, *Canon Christopher of St Aldate's, Oxford* (Abingdon: Abbey Press, 1967), p. 206.

Church of England would never have been reformed—without controversy it can never be kept reformed. Cranmer, Latimer & Ridley thought it worthwhile to die a cruel death to maintain the truths which are the subject of next Friday's evening Lecture in our Church.[1]

The causes of apostasy

1. The presence of numbers in the church with unrenewed hearts. We speak far less today than evangelicals used to do about people being 'professing Christians'. The term was intended to keep alive the awareness that we cannot be certain that all who seem to be believers, and who act like believers, are so in reality. As our Lord warns us in the Parable of the Sower and elsewhere, there are people who 'endure for a season' as temporary believers. In the parable of the Ten Virgins he puts half the number of those professing to be waiting for the coming of the Bridegroom in that category. Men may come under the power of the gospel; their lifestyle may change; their experience may be accompanied by a new happiness; they may even become active and eminent leaders in the churches, and yet at the last hear Christ say, 'I never knew you.' Scripture does not allow us to think of such persons as hypocrites, simply acting a part. On the contrary, their rejection will come as a surprise.

The Bible does not teach that any faith saves. Saving faith, the result of divine grace, is always accompanied by a changed heart. 'The faith of those chosen of God . . . is according to godliness' (*Titus* 1:1). Wherever there is 'faith' without regeneration it has to be that the uncured enmity of the natural man to spiritual things remains. Sometimes events will prove this to be the case. Where

[1] *Ibid.*, p. 213.

self still reigns—as in all men by nature—compromise will be the resort if persecution threatens. Or if some new teaching appears which promises popularity and success, it is likely to be received. How easily persuasive and impressive personalities, claiming to be exponents of Scripture, can draw numbers within the churches after them! This would not happen were it not true that for the unregenerate error has more appeal than truth. At the time 'many false prophets arise', Jesus says, 'many will fall away' (*Matt.* 24: 10, 11). The reason all do not fall away is that the real Christian has the saving illumination of the Holy Spirit in his heart.

2. *Unbelief.* This follows from the previous point. Where the heart is unrenewed, then unbelief exercises a secret power. This is not to say that the true Christian is without unbelief. On the contrary, every Christian has unbelief present in his life. It will be with us all our days. We cannot live as we want to do, or witness as we want to do, because we have unbelief at our heels. How then can we tell whether this unbelief is the result of an unregenerate heart or whether it is the relic of sin still present in the new man? One sure way to know the difference is whether we continue to take unbelief seriously. Scripture warns that unbelief is a very dangerous thing, and where it is not resisted it will overcome. This is a major theme of the Epistle to the Hebrews. The book was written to professing Jewish Christians who were being tempted to go back to Judaism. What was influencing them? It was unbelief. 'Take heed , brethren,'— be watchful, be very careful—'lest there be in any of you an evil heart of unbelief, in departing from the living God' (3:12). The children of Israel were excluded from the promised land because 'they believed not'; 'they could not enter in because of unbelief' (3:18, 19). The danger for the first

readers of this epistle was just the same. The essential preservative from apostasy is faith. 'Let us hold fast the profession of our faith without wavering.' The second half of Hebrews 10 details the peril of wavering, closing with the words: 'We are not of them who draw back unto perdition; but of them that believe to the saving of the soul.'

The true believer is the person, dissatisfied with himself, who sees his need of a stronger faith. As Spurgeon said: 'Some cry out against the Pope, and others against agnostics; but it is our own unbelief which is our worst enemy.'[1]

3. *An Abused Conscience*. Much is said in Scripture on maintaining a good conscience. Conscience is a God-given monitor; it is there to keep us awake, to remind us of our need to fear God who will be our judge. A Christian with a good conscience can speak with Paul of, 'knowing the fear of the Lord'. Paul, called to defend himself before Felix, has a greater concern: 'I exercise myself to have always a conscience void of offence toward God, and men' (*Acts* 24:16). In giving instruction to Timothy, Paul makes it plain that failure in the right use of conscience is the pathway to apostasy. In 1 Timothy 1:5, 6 he speaks of 'a good conscience and faith unfeigned: from which some having swerved have turned aside unto vain jangling.' The Christian warfare, he goes on to say, means, 'Holding faith, and a good conscience; which some having put away concerning faith have made shipwreck.' Later in the same letter he speaks of those in the latter time who shall depart from the faith, 'having their conscience seared with a hot iron'. Sin has silenced conscience. By way of

---

[1] *Metropolitan Tabernacle Pulpit*, vol. 36, p. 378.

contrast, Paul speaks of true servants of Christ as those who 'hold the mystery of the faith in a pure conscience' (*1 Tim.* 3:9). A tender conscience is a conscience that fears sin. 'Let everyone that names the name of Christ depart from iniquity' (*2 Tim.* 2:19).

4. Satanic intervention. Christians gave to the Emperor Julian the title 'the Apostate', but that title belongs most truly to the Devil, a great 'angel of light' who 'fell from heaven' (*Luke* 10:18). 'We wrestle not against flesh and blood, but against principalities and powers', and the great object of these evil powers is to draw men away from God, and especially to draw those who have professed faith in Christ. He comes with many devices and in many disguises, but the object is always the same. Satan knows that men are kept to salvation through belief of the truth; therefore, if the truth can be corrupted or denied an apostasy is bound to follow. To that end a flood of falsehoods proceed out of his mouth. The purpose is to cause men to listen to 'seducing spirits and doctrines of demons' (*1 Tim.* 4:1) Scripture warns us that unless we are watchful we will fail to recognize what lies behind the words of men: 'Beloved, believe not every spirit, but try the spirits whether they are of God: because many false prophets are gone out into the world' (*1 John* 4:1).

We underestimate the influence of Satan at our peril. No one is exempt from his tempting power. One might suppose that preachers who have the privilege of being constant students of the word of God, and who are surrounded day by day with spiritual concerns, would have no problem in detecting demonic temptation. But it is very possible for faith to be undermined while we are engaged in ministry to others. Imperceptibly convictions may weaken, love to Christ may cool, and instead of the expectations we once had there may be the mere formality of a routine. An orthodox ministry may remain in public, while temptation to backsliding and apostasy has got entrance into the heart.

Christian history does not lack evidence of this possibility.

> It is recorded of the German Baur, that in youth he was full of evangelical zeal. He came into contact with Strauss, and gradually the spiritual life went from him. Unbelief took the place of faith. He found he could not even pray; and when his wife was dying he had to send for an earnest pastor in the neighbourhood to pray with her, and supply his lack of service. He found himself dumb in the presence of his dying wife. Unbelief could do nothing for him. It had closed his lips; and it had hidden the face of God.[1]

The life of Baur should point us to one of the greatest contemporary dangers in the churches. Baur spent his life as a professor of theology at Tubingen, and he was at the head of a movement that removed the recognition of the supernatural in theological education. That movement was to have catastrophic effects not simply in Germany, but in Britain and in the United States. So-called academic theology has no need of prayer or of the Holy Spirit; the promotion of spiritual life is not its object. Dr Oliver Barclay, who understands the university scene as well as anyone in Britain today, has written recently: 'No university in Britain would now boast that for them "the fear of the Lord is the beginning of wisdom". One wonders if any university theological department could rightly claim that motto today.'[2]

This situation in the universities has been discussed by Dr John H. Leith, a man who also gave his life to theological

---

[1] H. Bonar, *Our Ministry*, pp. 56-7. Ferdinand Christian Baur (1792–1860).

[2] Oliver Barclay, *Evangelicalism in Britain*, p. 131.

education. Shortly before he died in 2002 he wrote an important book that fell virtually unnoticed from the press, *Crisis in
the Church: The Plight of Theological Education*. He noted that,
'Fifty years ago departments of Bible in church colleges taught
courses not simply to instruct or to encourage discussion but to
enhance Christian life in the church.' That this is no longer the
case Leith attributed chiefly to university influence: 'Today', he
says, 'College courses in religion taught in a value neutral context
. . . undermine the life of the church more than they build it up.
In fact the university context is seldom neutral. It may actually
be anti-Christian, and Christian texts may be interpreted by a
"hermeneutics" of suspicion. This influence has changed the very
nature of theological seminaries. The task of the seminary is not
to produce church historians, professional theologians, or techni-
cal biblical scholars. The first task is to prepare preachers who use
theological and biblical knowledge to proclaim the gospel and to
nurture congregations.' Leith was not exaggerating when he went
on to talk about 'the tragedy of seminary life today'.[1]

If apostasy is to be effectually countered in our nation today
then churches need to stop giving any honour to a system that
serves unbelief. At the heart of the system lies the Satanic temptation to pride in man's knowledge and reason.[2]

---

[1] John H. Leith, *Crisis in the Church* (Louisville, KY: Westminster John Knox
Press, 1997), pp. 19-21.

[2] In speaking of pride as a source of apostasy, John Owen wrote of those 'who
submit Scripture, and everything contained in it, to the judgment and sentence of
their own reason . . . Hence it is that all those doctrines of the gospel which have
anything of spiritual mystery in them, and so not absolutely reconcilable unto
reason as corrupt and carnal, are by many so laden with contempt and scorn that
it is sufficient to expose any man unto the contumelies of "ignorant, irrational, and

5. The judgment of God as a cause of apostasy. When we see, as we do today, much evidence of apostasy we are prone to question why God does not act. But Scripture does not allow us to think in such a way. In a scene of apostasy God *is* acting. When people have the light of knowledge of Christ, and despise it, God may give them over to hardness of heart. In John 12:37-40 we read, 'But though he had done so many miracles before them, yet they believed not on him . . . therefore they could not believe, because that Isaiah said again, He has blinded their eyes, and hardened their heart; that they should not see with their eyes, nor understand with their heart, and be converted.' Those who once enjoyed light thus find it taken away. In speaking of the great apostasy described in 2 Thessalonians 2, we read God 'sends them strong delusion, that they may believe a lie'. John Owen wrote:

> When a people, a nation, a church, or private persons, have received the gospel and the profession thereof, not walking answerably thereunto, God may forsake them, and withdraw from them the means of their edification and preservation.[1]

This removal of God's presence has special reference to the work of the Holy Spirit. The Holy Spirit is the guardian of spiritual truth and life; it is only by his power that we can believe, only by his anointing that we can see. The gospel cannot be preserved without him. After speaking of 'the form of sound words', Paul says to Timothy, 'that good thing that was committed to you keep by the Holy Spirit who dwells in us' (2 Tim. 1:14). Without him, whatever we do, there will be no keeping, but declension

---

foolish", who dares to avow them.' *Nature and Causes of Apostasy from the Gospel, Works,* vol. 7, p. 132.

[1] Owen, *Works,* vol. 7, p. 141.

will be certain, and it may be final. The most serious sin known in Scripture is that of doing 'despite to the Spirit of grace', that is, so provoking him to leave us that the case is hopeless, as we read of in Hebrews 10.

In this connection an article by Daniel Steele, an American Methodist of the nineteenth century, is very relevant. Under the title, 'The Holy Spirit the Conservator of Orthodoxy', he argued that churches inevitably fall when they dishonour the Holy Spirit, and then flounder as they attempt to find substitutes for what they have lost. 'What was the first step', he asked, 'which led down from Puritanism to Atheism in New England? It was the attempt to build up a Church without the Holy Spirit in conviction of sin, in regeneration and sanctification. An orthodox creed must perish when the spiritual life dies out of a denomination, and heresies will swarm into the vacuum left by the Holy Ghost.'

This scene he saw being repeated in his own day. The strength of Methodism had been the presence of the Spirit of God. Now he saw a great change:

> There was no place for evangelists in Methodism fifty years ago, because every preacher preached the whole Gospel, thundered the terrors of the Lord into the ears of slumbering sinners. How rarely now do we hear a sermon on the second coming of Christ, and the day of judgment! This style of preaching is out of fashion in our pulpits, just as though the everlasting gospel of Christ were subject to capricious fashion . . . If the convert is troubled with doubts, instead of being pointed to the fullness of the Spirit as the source of assurance, he is told that doubts trouble everybody and to plunge into Christian work so earnestly as to forget your doubts. Thus the Holy Spirit is insensibly supplanted. What will be the outcome of all this? The fervent and high spiritual era of

> Methodism will pass away; then look out for the speculative era
> to come; the era of doctrinal disintegration, theological confusion
> and schism.[1]

This prediction of what would happen was not a guess. When the gracious influences of the Holy Spirit are withdrawn apostasy is sure to follow.

Duties in a time of apostasy

1. An awareness of the danger of false teaching needs reviving. An easy-going, false charity is the spirit of the age; we are all subject to its influence and life will be far more comfortable for those who accept it as progress. But we need to remember that no great spiritual advance has ever been made where that spirit has been accepted by the churches. Peaceful times, the absence of controversy, and calm opinions may all be desirable, but it was not for these things that Christians were described as those that had 'turned the world upside down' (*Acts* 17:6), and as a sect 'everywhere spoken against' (*Acts* 28:22). So it has always been when the fear of man is scorned and the gospel is proclaimed in power. Those who contend for the faith, warn against false teachers (however exalted they may be), and sacrifice all for the truth's sake, and do not belong to the class of whom Jesus says, 'Woe unto you, when all men shall speak well of you!' (*Luke* 6:26). Rather, as George Whitefield found, 'To be a Christian is to be a scandal.' Sometimes it will mean, as in his case, standing for evangelical truth when few are prepared to do so.

In the apostasy of the 1670s Owen pointed out how the 'public scorn cast on important evangelical truths' had the tendency to

[1] *Experience: A Quarterly Journal*, vol. 4, 1887–8 (London: Peter Thompson), p. 214.

prevent men openly contending for them. And he listed particular factors liable to make orthodox men neglect their duty: 'Sloth, self-love, carnal fears, earthly ambitious designs.'[1]

2. Strong emphasis is needed on progress in the Christian life as the only sure preservative against apostasy. This is the lesson taught in the Epistle to the Hebrews. Where lay the danger of the Jews who professed Christ? It was that they were children in their understanding; they were like babes still only able to receive a diet of milk (*Heb.* 5:12). They had not got beyond being spiritual beginners, and this was a dangerous condition. If they stayed in that state there would be no way of telling whether they were truly regenerate Christians or only temporary believers. Hence the urgency of the exhortation: 'Therefore leaving the principles of the doctrine of Christ, let us go on unto perfection' (or 'to maturity', the better translation of modern versions of *Heb.* 6:1). A person has not arrived when they profess conversion; if their new life is real there must be growth, especially in faith; there must be increasing knowledge of Christ and particularly of his present exaltation and heavenly glory. The possession of a superficial Christianity will prove no preservative when apostasy has to be faced. Calvin warns teachers: 'In urging men to perfection we must not toil slowly or listlessly, much less give up.'[2] There is a maturity to be reached in this life even though it may only be called a partial perfection. For as Calvin also says, 'The highest perfection of the godly in this life is an earnest desire to make progress.'[3]

[1] Owen, *Works,* vol. 7, p. 245.
[2] *Institutes,* 4:1:20.
[3] Calvin, commenting on *Eph.* 3:16.

Our evangelical predecessors were stronger than we are in urging the nature and necessity of holiness of life. It is possible for evangelicals to be too exclusively concerned with evangelism and conversion. There has been a tendency to preach as though 'decisions for Christ' are guarantees of 'successful' churches. But Calvinistic belief can also be a danger at this point. In our desire to assert the once-for-all nature of regeneration, and the certainty that the elect cannot perish, we may lead young disciples to suppose they will never face the danger of apostasy. But that is not how the New Testament addresses professing Christians. Paul himself had to guard against being 'a castaway' (*1 Cor.* 9:27). John Owen asked his hearers, 'Brethren and sisters, how do you know but you and I may fall?'[1] The balance of our teaching is seriously wrong if it induces any kind of carelessness. A kind of carefree Antinomianism is a prevalent danger in evangelical circles today, and if Calvinism gets mixed with Antinomianism it can be a deadly combination.

The New Testament knows nothing of a Christianity devoid of godly fear. To be a subject of divine grace entails living 'with fear and trembling' (*Phil.* 2:12). 'The comfort of the Holy Spirit' and 'walking in the fear of the Lord' belong together (*Acts* 9:31). The only way to glory is the path of holiness, 'without which no man shall see the Lord' (*Heb.* 12:14). 'Let us have grace', the argument in Hebrews concludes, 'whereby we may serve God acceptably with reverence and godly fear: for our God is a consuming fire' (*Heb.* 12:28, 29). As John Murray writes on Romans 11:22: 'There is no security in the bond of the gospel apart from perseverance. There

---

[1] Owen, *Works,* vol. 9, p. 334.

is no such thing as continuance in the favour of God in spite of apostasy; God's saving embrace and endurance are correlative.'[1]

A striking difference between the leading Puritan authors and much contemporary evangelical literature is the absence of attention to the fear of God.[2]

3. Maintain private and personal communion with Christ. Apostasy commonly begins where attention moves away from the inner spiritual life. 'Take heed unto thyself', is Paul's command to Timothy, 'and unto the doctrine; continue in them: for in doing this thou shalt both save thyself, and them that hear thee' (*1 Tim.* 4:16). For all Christians fellowship with Christ is to come before all public duties. Peter's confirmation of love to Christ goes before the command, 'Feed my sheep' (*John* 21:15-17). The Saviour charged the church at Ephesus with forgetting this priority (*Rev.* 2:4).

Calvin, speaking of what it is to 'possess and enjoy Christ as our Saviour', wrote:

> This deserves our careful attention. Most people consider fellow-ship with Christ, and believing in Christ, to be the same thing;

[1] John Murray, *Epistle to the Romans* (Grand Rapids: Eerdmans, 1965), vol. 2, p. 88. He writes: 'Christian piety is constantly aware of the perils to faith, of the danger of coming short, and is characterized by the fear and trembling which the high demands of God's calling constrain (*cf. 1 Cor.* 2:3; *Phil.* 2:12; *Heb.* 4:1: *1 Pet.* 1:17). "Let him that thinketh he standeth take heed lest he fall" (*1 Cor.* 10:12).'

[2] See, for example, John Bunyan, *Works* (Edinburgh: The Banner of Truth Trust, 1991), vol. 3, p. 159, where the fear of the Lord is called 'the pulse of the soul'. This true fear is marked by 'saving convictions of sin, laying fast hold of Christ for salvation, begetting and continuing in the soul a great reverence for God, his word, and ways, keeping it tender, and making it afraid to turn from them, in anything that may dishonour God, break its peace, grieve the Spirit, or cause the enemy to speak reproachfully.'

but the fellowship which we have with Christ is the consequence of faith. In a word, faith is not a distant view, but a warm embrace, of Christ, by which he dwells within us, and we are filled with the Divine Spirit.[1]

Such fellowship cannot be real in public unless it begins in secret. The private precedes and determine the public (*Matt.* 6:6). As John Flavel noted long ago, 'Observed duties maintain our credit, but secret duties maintain our life.'[2] Yet too often this connection is missed. When the declension was spreading rapidly in the churches of Britain, comparatively few saw the problem as did Daniel Lamont of Edinburgh, who wrote: 'The secret of the Church's comparative failure lies in the eclipse of the individual prayer life. It is to be feared that a host of people who still give formal assent to the truth of Christianity do not cultivate an inner life with God.'[3] This testimony to what lies hidden behind backsliding and apostasy has the concurrence of Christian leaders across the centuries.[4]

Where fellowship with God is real, one mark of it will be felt, personal sorrow when unbelief gains ground in the church and

---

[1] *Commentaries on Galatians and Ephesians* (Edinburgh: Calvin Translation Society, 1854), p. 262. In speaking of the insufficiency of 'believing in Christ' he is speaking of nominal rather than saving faith.

[2] Flavel, *Works,* vol. 5, p. 520.

[3] D. Lamont, *The Anchorage of Life* (London: Inter-Varsity, 1946), p. 209.

[4] Bunyan, enumerating steps to apostasy, writes: 'They cast off by degrees private duties, as closet prayer, curbing their lusts, watching, sorrow for sin, and the like.' *Pilgrim's Progress* (Edinburgh: The Banner of Truth Trust, 2009), p. 177. Charles Hodge, likewise identifies 'neglect of fellowship with God' with 'neglect of the more private duties of religion.' *Princeton Sermons* (Edinburgh: The Banner of Truth Trust, 2011), pp. 112-3.

world (*Psa.* 119:136; *Ezek.* 9:4). Spurgeon was not speaking as a preacher but as a Christian when he said:

> O friends, I know not how you feel about the prevailing skepticism of the age, but I am heart-sick of it! I shun the place where I am likely to hear the utterances of men who do not tremble at God's word. I turn away from the multitude of books which advocate doubt and error. The evil is too painful for me. If I knew my mother's name would be defamed in certain company, I would keep out of it; if I knew my father's character would be trailed in the mire, I would travel far not to hear a sound so offensive. I could wish to be deaf and blind, rather than hear or read the modern falsehoods which, at this time, so often wound my spirit.[1]

4. Dependence on the Atoning Death of Christ alone. I said at the outset there is a radical difference between a temporary back-slider and one who died apostate. One has the principle of eternal life within, the other does not. One is being kept for salvation, the other is not. But it is not the consciousness of being in the right category that is the most vital thing. A child of God may sometimes fear he is no Christian at all, while the person who is not destined for heaven may believe that he is (*Isa.* 50:10, 11). The truth is that all Christians are sinners still; failures, omissions, and unworthiness are abiding realities. Of sinners Paul continued to say, 'I am chief' (*1 Tim.* 1:16). It is not feelings that determine our status and safety; it is dependence on Christ's blood—'the blood

---

[1] *Metropolitan Tabernacle Pulpit,* vol. 35, pp. 100-1. 'Is it nothing unto us that so many nations in the world, where the profession of the gospel and an avowed subjection of the soul and conscience unto Jesus Christ did flourish for some ages, are now utterly overrun with Mohammedanism, paganism, and atheism?' Owen, *Works,* vol. 7, p. 242.

of the everlasting covenant' (*Heb.* 13:20). The sinner for whom Christ died is as accepted by God as surely as the Son of God is himself accepted. For a season the true Christian may lose sight of the cross, but he will come back to the sight and to 'Jesus Christ, the righteous, the propitiation for our sins'. 'He that eateth my flesh, and drinketh my blood, has eternal life' (*John* 6:54). 'We are not of them who draw back unto perdition; but of them that believe to the saving of the soul' (*Heb.* 10:39).

The cross of Christ is the ground of the believer's assurance. It was for C. H. Spurgeon in the Downgrade controversy shortly before his death. He closed a letter of February 16, 1889, with these words:

> The Lord is faithful, whatever men may be. Let us trust in him, and not be afraid. Into the thick darkness that now hovers over much of the church, and blinds many of her leaders, we advance with uplifted banner, believing that the gloom will vanish before the eternal light. *Crux Lux*. The doctrine of the cross is light. This we will uphold until death.[1]

---

[1] *Metropolitan Tabernacle Pulpit*, 35:108.

4

THE BENEFITS AND DANGERS OF CONTROVERSY[1]

J. Gresham Machen once wrote: 'If we are going to avoid controversy, we might as well close our Bibles; for the New Testament is a controversial book practically from beginning to the end.' Then he made this prediction about the future:

> I do not know all the things that will happen when the great revival sweeps over the Church, the great revival for which we long. Certainly I do not know *when* that revival will come; its coming stands in the Spirit's power. But about one thing that will happen when that blessing comes I think we can be fairly sure. When a great and true revival comes in the Church, the present miserable, feeble talk about avoidance of controversy on the part of the servants of Jesus Christ will all be swept away as with a mighty flood.[2]

You understand that in speaking of revival, Machen was not speaking simply of a time of blessing or excitement in a local church; he was referring to the kind of awakening in the churches and in society which turns attention to God, brings conviction of sin, humbles people, and even changes the course of history. But

[1] An address delivered at the Leicester Conference, 28 April, 2012.
[2] J. G. Machen, *What is Christianity?*, p. 220.

111

is his prediction, that such an event will be accompanied by controversy, justified? I believe that it is. Church history shows that all the great turning points in history have been times of controversy and there is good reason why that is the case. It is because every great advance of the kingdom of God takes place in conjunction with the recovery of biblical truth, and when the truth is known in its power opposition will not be absent. Thus when the book of Acts tells us, 'The word of God grew and multiplied', we go on to read that the Christians were seen as a 'sect' and 'everywhere spoken against' (*Acts* 28: 22).

Before we speak of the benefits of controversy, I note three examples of controversies that marked turning points in history.

1. The great Reformation of the sixteenth century. There are those today who think that the Reformation, and the division that gave rise to the Protestant churches, were things that might have been avoided. There ought, it is said, to have been more tolerance and less passion on both sides. The differences, they believe, were more over words than over fundamental issues. Such spokesmen concede that some Reformation of the church was necessary, but suggest that it might have been carried on peacefully had there been better mutual understanding.

This argument overlooks something: there were people who thought in just that kind of way at the time of the Reformation. Erasmus, the Renaissance Dutch scholar, is their best representative. Erasmus believed in the need for the Bible to be translated and known; and he supported the reform of abuses in the church. At the same time he thought that all this might be achieved peacefully by a cautious policy of education. So he complained that Martin Luther was a threat to the peace and unity of the church;

the German reformer was too dogmatic—he treated opinions, and 'doubtful and unnecessary' beliefs, as though they were certainties. Erasmus blamed Luther for his 'delight in assertions'.

It was to this thinking of Erasmus that Luther replied in *The Bondage of the Will,* a book which showed that Erasmus was not a real believer in the doctrines of the Bible at all. The Dutchman's thinking, Luther wrote, meant regarding

> Christian doctrines as nothing better than the opinions of philosophers and men: and that it is the greatest folly to quarrel about, contend for, and assert them, as nothing can arise therefrom but contention and the disturbance of the public peace.[1]

He replied to Erasmus:

> Allow us to be assertors, and to study and delight in assertions: and do you favour your Sceptics and Academics until Christ shall have called you also. The Holy Spirit is not a Sceptic, nor are what he has written in our hearts doubts or opinions, but assertions more certain, and more firm, than life itself.[2]

Erasmus, Luther says, made keeping peace of 'greater consideration than salvation, than the word of God, than the glory of Christ', and the cause of his mistake was that his viewpoint was fundamentally different from that of the Reformers. He saw the controversy over the Reformation as a difference between men. For Luther it was much more than that: it was a movement of the Spirit of God. Men were called to take part but God was the

---

[1] *The Bondage of the Will* (Grand Rapids and London: Eerdmans and SGU, 1931), p. 23 A new translation was edited by J. I. Packer and O. R. Johnston (Cambridge: Clarke, 1957).

[2] *Ibid.,* p. 24.

true agent. In the words of John Knox, 'God gave his Holy Spirit to simple men in great abundance.' In essence, the Reformation was a revival. God sent forth light and truth, and the hostility that erupted was exactly what Scripture warns us to expect. The uproar in the sixteenth century did not come about because of 'opinions'; it came from enmity to the Bible and to God. 'The carnal mind is enmity against God; for it is not subject to the law of God, neither indeed can be' (*Rom.* 8:7).

2. *The Evangelical Revival of the eighteenth century,* or as it became known in the American colonies, 'The Great Awakening'. This also was attended by controversy, not now between Protestants and Roman Catholics but between Protestants themselves. Yet the issue was very similar to the main issue at the Reformation. The devil's constant strategy is to seek to merge the church and the world so that the people of God lose their distinctiveness and be no longer as 'a city set upon a hill'. The primary way for Satan to achieve this is to confuse what it means to be a Christian. He uses false prophets to make entrance into the kingdom of God broad and not narrow, and so becoming a Christian is just a matter of belonging to the institutional church. 'Be baptized, profess Christianity, attend church', and that is all. This was largely the position on both sides of the Atlantic in the eighteenth century, as it had been two centuries earlier. When Whitefield and Wesley began to preach the necessity of being born again people heard it as though it was a new religion. Typical was the testimony of Thomas Webb, a parish clerk in England, who had listened to many sermons in his lifetime, and yet confessed, 'The new birth, justification by faith only, the want of free will in man to do good works without the special grace to God, was as it were,

a new language to me.'[1] Archibald Alexander, who was brought up among Presbyterians in the Shenandoah Valley, says the same thing. The day came in his life when, away from home, a Baptist millwright asked him

> Whether I had experience the new birth. I hesitated and said, 'Not that I know of.' 'Ah', said he, 'if you had ever experienced this change you would know something about it!' Here the conversation ended; but it led me to think more seriously whether there were any such change. It seemed to be in the Bible; but I thought there must be some method of explaining it away; for among the Presbyterians I had never heard of anyone who had experienced the new birth, nor could I recollect ever to have heard it mentioned.[2]

The fundamental controversy in the eighteenth-century revival was about the nature of vital, life-changing Christianity. The evangelicals appealed to the testimony of the New Testament on such truths as the power of the Holy Spirit in conviction of sin, and his work in giving assurance of salvation, and they were told such things were no longer necessary in 'Christian' countries. It was 'fanaticism' and highly offensive to preach to churchgoers as though they might not be Christians.

Take one particular instance of this controversy. Jonathan Edwards, leader in the Awakening in colonial America, was

---

[1] *George Whitefield's Journals* (Edinburgh: The Banner of Truth Trust, 1985), p. 327. He writes that it was his sermon on the 'Nature and Necessity of our Regeneration or the New Birth', which under God began the awakening at London, Bristol, Gloucester and Gloucestershire. *Ibid.*, p. 86.

[2] James W. Alexander, *Life of Archibald Alexander* (New York: Charles Scribner, 1854), p. 41.

dismissed from the church at Northampton which he had served for twenty-three years. The cause of his dismissal was that he had come to see the wrongness of allowing churchgoers to come to the Lord's Table although they could give no testimony to their personal faith in Christ. When he sought to persuade his people that the Lord's Table, and the purity of the church, needed to be guarded, there was such an outcry against him that it terminated his ministry.

3. *The Modern Controversy over Scripture.* In the last century practically all the historic denominations of the English-speaking nations, from America to New Zealand, fell into serious decline. Whole communities where light once burned brightly were left in darkness. This happened because the leadership in these churches took the wrong side in controversy over whether the whole Bible is God-given revelation which is to be obeyed in all it says.

Now although this controversy continues to be contemporary, we are all aware that it did not begin yesterday. It came out into the light in the 1880s, and it was at its height until about the 1920s, when tragically the mainline churches in our countries gave in to the teaching that the Bible contains both truth and error. The majority argued that this change of belief was simply the inevitable result of a better understanding of the nature of the Bible. No one should be disturbed about this discovery, they said, because faith does not rest upon a Book but upon the living Christ. The claim was, 'It is Christ we worship, not a book!'

Such was a common way in which falsehood was presented and it was promised that there was no danger in accepting it. After all, they said, there is a difference between believing the Bible and 'believing in theories about the Bible'. The historic Christian belief in the inerrancy of all Scripture was only 'a theory' produced to explain its composition. Other possible explanations were not to be excluded. In 1888 a prominent English Baptist leader, John Clifford, defended this thinking in a major speech which he entitled 'The Battle of the Sacred Books'.[1] 'Books' in the plural was central to his thesis. There are other 'sacred books'; Christianity cannot be exclusive in its claim to have revelation from heaven. The Bible is only 'superior revelation', but in saying this, he added, 'Let me carefully note that we speak of the Bible ITSELF, and not of any human theories concerning its composition.' Without stating whom he was attacking, Clifford referred to those of orthodox belief as 'scholastic system-builders, and priest-bitten ecclesiastics'. They are people, he said, who think 'geography and statistics as equally vital with redemption and ethics'—a veiled way of saying that if matters of fact are wrong in the Bible that should not trouble us. It is, he said, 'fatal' to forget 'that our faith does not rest, in its last support, upon the qualities and forces of the Scriptures, but on God . . . Jesus did not say to His disciples, "Go, preach to everybody, everywhere, and lo, a book is with you; but, lo, I am with you." Our trust is in a living Leader; not in a book we read.'

Clifford was only repeating an idea already becoming popular and supposedly the result of the progress of scholarship. It was thirty-six years after his speech that a document called the Auburn Affirmation was published in the United States, signed by 150 Presbyterian ministers and then by others until the number grew to about 1,300. This Affirmation claimed that men of

[1] I have written more fully on this controversy in *Archibald G. Brown: Spurgeon's Successor* (Edinburgh: The Banner of Truth Trust, 2011).

liberal belief in their theology had the same right to be in pulpits as traditionalists. They all 'believed the Bible', it was just 'certain theories concerning the inspiration of the Bible' over which they differed.

But by the 1920s the distinction between the Bible and 'theories' was worked out more widely. It was now said that one could believe in the cross of Christ without accepting any 'theory' of the atonement. Or one could believe in 'the resurrection of Christ' without determining whether it was a bodily resurrection. Bodily resurrection was only a 'theory', and the liberals were equally entitled to their theories.[1]

In some great controversies the leaders on the side of truth are not always seen to win in their lifetimes. It was so in this controversy. The two foremost leaders in opposition to liberal theology were C. H. Spurgeon in Britain, and J. Gresham Machen in America. Both men saw the tide go against them. Spurgeon saw a majority failing to support his call for subscription to a definite creed, and Machen was suspended by the Presbyterian Church, after a heroic defence of the faith. Both men died in their mid-fifties. Books by other faithful men have since demonstrated that the position defended by Spurgeon and Machen is the position taken by Scripture itself. Yet these books were largely ignored. What cannot be ignored is the providence of God in bringing spiritual

---

[1] Commenting on the Auburn Affirmation, Gresham Machen wrote, 'A document which will affirm the resurrection but will not say that our Lord rose from the dead with the same body in which He suffered—this is simply one more manifestation of that destructive Modernism which is the deadliest enemy of the Christian religion in practically all the larger churches of the world at the present day.' *Modernism and the Board of Foreign Missions of the Presbyterian Church in the USA,* (1933), pp. 23-4.

desolation in all the denominations where the unbelief of liberalism was accepted. Once fruitful churches became a wilderness. Disbelief cannot coexist with the sanction of the Holy Spirit.

The benefits of controversy

That great blessings may result from controversies is an evident lesson of history.

1. Controversy leads to closer and clearer definitions of the truth. The great creeds and confessions of the churches have been born out of controversies. Heresies that might have ended Christian testimony have been overruled to establish the truth more brightly. In the year 1555 error had come in like a flood in England, and those who opposed it were being put to death in numbers. Yet when Hugh Latimer died at the stake, October 16, 1555, he could say to his fellow martyr, 'Be of good comfort, Master Ridley, and play the man. We shall this day light such a candle by God's grace in England, as I trust shall never be put out.' His belief that controversy and persecution would be overruled for good was correct. 'There must be divisions among you', Paul told the church at Corinth, 'that those approved may become more manifest' (*1 Cor.* 11:19). As Charles Hodge says: 'It is a great consolation to know that dissensions . . . are not fortuitous, but are ordered by the providence of God, and are designed, as storms, for the purpose of purification.' Or, in the words of the Puritan, Samuel Bolton: 'God suffers errors to arise to bring us back to the original word of God, that there we might rectify all. If there had not been such clashing and disputing in former ages, our way had not been clear to us, in many glorious truths.'[1]

[1] 'They that purify silver to the purpose, use to put it in the fire again and again,

Jonathan Edwards' sufferings at Northampton had the same consequence. They were not in vain. More attention came to be given to the need for a credible evidence of a change of heart in order to permit admittance to the Lord's Supper, and this led to a very general change in practice of many churches.[1]

Judged in purely numerical terms, the decline of the mainline churches into liberalism a hundred years ago was a tragedy, but it prompted many faithful men and women at home and on the mission fields to take a stronger stand on the inerrancy of Scripture.

2. *Controversy has brought divisions that are a blessing to the world.* There are times in history when the call of Hebrews 13:13 is again appropriate: 'Let us go forth therefore unto him without the camp, bearing his reproach.' First-century Christians were to leave a dead Judaism; they belonged to the Jerusalem 'which is above,' outside the Jerusalem which 'is in bondage with her children' (*Gal.* 4:25, 26). The call to separation is sometimes the call of God.

---

that it may be thoroughly tried. So is the truth of God; there is scarce any truth but hath been tried over and over again, and still if any dross happen to mingle with it, then God calls it in question again. If in former times there have been Scriptures alleged that have not been pertinent to prove it, that truth shall into the fire again, that what is dross may be burnt up; the Holy Ghost is so curious, so delicate, so exact, He cannot bear that falsehood should be mingled with the truth of the Gospel.' Thomas Goodwin, quoted by James Stalker, *Imago Christi* (London: Hodder and Stoughton, 1893), pp. 292-3.

[1] See Charles Hodge, *Systematic Theology,* vol. 3 (London and Edinburgh: Nelson, 1874), p. 569. In Thomas Murphy's valuable book, *The Presbytery of the Log College; or, The Cradle of the Presbyterian Church in America* (Philadelphia, 1889), p. 180, he lists the settling of the right conditions for admission to the Lord's Supper as one of the results of the eighteenth-century revival.

It is true that there have been times when earnest resistance to error in a denomination has been owned of God for its recovery, but there are also times when believers have to find spiritual life outside churches that are dead. There are religious institutions where believers have remained even after all attempts at recovery have proved futile.[1] Those who did not leave the Presbyterian Church with Machen were to find this. Henry Coray, a witness of the 1930s' controversy, commented on that point fifty years later: 'One is constrained to look back and ask the question, "How goes the battle?" The answer had to be: the battle is over and the mopping up process is going on. The warriors have sheathed their swords. Where is there in the (now) United Presbyterian Church a single rallying point, a stalwart uncompromising post where the conflict is raging?'[2]

Certainly, as I will argue, divisions arising out of controversy are not always beneficial, but both the Reformation and the eighteenth-century Awakening demonstrate the great blessings that have come to nations in times of disruption. It is not romanticising history to say that vast benefits, spiritual, moral, and economic, followed the Reformation: society was uplifted, tyrannies put down, and freedom of speech established.

Dangers

1. The danger of Christians not recognising when serious controversy is justified and when it is not. I believe that the three

---

[1] See N. B. Stonehouse, *J. Gresham Machen, A Biographical Memoir* (Grand Rapids: Eerdmans, 1955), p. 310.

[2] Henry W. Coray, *J. Gresham Machen, A Silhouette* (Grand Rapids; Kregel, 1981), pp. 111-2.

controversies noted above warranted controversy and division. The truths involved were fundamental and worth suffering for. We are commanded to 'contend earnestly for the faith once delivered to the saints'. But that does not mean we are to contend over every difference that arises. There are fundamental truths, lesser truths and matters which belong more to the sphere of speculation. If the line between these is not correctly drawn then great damage is liable to be done. The understanding of the best of men remains imperfect, and that means that a determination to secure or insist on unanimity in all things, will only multiply disputes and divisions. There are many instances where this has happened in church history, when the kingdom of God has been injured by believers engaging in disputes among themselves on issues not fundamental. This was part of the reason why the Puritan movement in England lost its ascendency. Men like-minded on the gospel fell out over the issue of how the church is to be governed. Now that is not a trivial subject. The Bible speaks on church government. But godly men differ on how parts of the biblical teaching are to be interpreted. The difference between those of Presbyterian and Independent views weakened their whole cause. In the last sermons Puritans preached before they were put out of their churches in 1662, there are pleas for more brotherly love, but by that date much damage had been done.[1]

[1] Thomas Watson's probably last morning sermon to his congregation in 1662 was on 'A new commandment give I unto you.' On the same date one of the 'legacies' left by Thomas Brooks to his people was: 'Labour mightily for a healing spirit. This legacy I would leave with you as a matter of great concernment. Away with all discriminating names whatever, that may hinder the applying of balm to heal your wounds. Discord and division become no Christian; for wolves to harry the lambs, is no wonder; but for one lamb to worry another, this is unnatural

Or consider what happened among Bible-believing Presbyterians in the United States in the 1930s. Those who rallied round Machen formed a new denomination, but it was to split over such questions as unfulfilled prophecy, and whether the wine drunk at the Lord's Supper should be alcoholic. Again these points are not incidental, but they were claimed to justify the breaking of fellowship between men who had stood together on fundamental truths.

If good men, as these men were, failed to draw the distinction between first and secondary truths, and between mistakes which are tolerable and errors which are not, it underlines the difficulty that often enters into controversy. One lesson to be drawn is that not all Christians are called to be engaged in controversy. To play a useful part in a controversy means being a teacher of others, and Scripture is clear, not all Christians are called to teach: 'Let not many of you become teachers, my brethren' (*James* 3:1). For a start that rules out women taking any lead in controversies. Others are also ruled out. While all are called to be faithful, not even all teachers are gifted for controversy. Some may be eminent in one sphere but not in this one. It was an old Methodist who once

---

and monstrous. God hath made his wrath to smoke against us for the divisions and heart-burnings that have been amongst us. Labour for oneness in love and affection with everyone that is one with Christ; let their forms be what they will: that which wins most Christ's heart, should win most with ours, and that is his own grace and holiness.' Baxter wrote to John Eliot in 1668, 'Twenty years long we prayed peace and unity but lived as a peace hating generation.' Puritan authors addressing this subject include: Jeremiah Burroughs, *Irenicum, To the Lovers of Truth and Peace. Heart Divisions Opened* (1646); Richard Baxter, *The Cure of Church Divisions*, 1670; and John Howe, 'The Carnality of Religious Contentions' in *Works,* vol. 3 (London: Tegg, 1848).

said that the Methodists are good for leading sinners to Christ but no good in controversy. John Duncan, speaking about the early church Fathers, said, 'The primitive Fathers were very poor divines. I don't think Polycarp could have stood a theological examination by John Owen; but he was a famous man to burn.' That is to say, God qualified Polycarp for what he was called to be, a martyr for Christ.[1] This is not an argument to justify theological pacificism, yet it needs to be said that not all are called to be leaders in controversy. Unhappily it has too often been that men of a contentious spirit have taken this role for themselves.[2]

2. *The danger of being distracted from what is of first importance.* Potential controversies are ever present and it is easy to become participants. The warnings of Scripture are relevant to this phenomenon: we are told not 'to pay attention to myths and endless genealogies' that lead to 'fruitless discussion' (*1 Tim.* 1:4, 6). 'Avoid foolish controversies and genealogies and strife and disputes about the Law, for they are unprofitable and worthless' (*Titus* 3:9). The nature of the controversies to which Paul refers is not clear; what is clear is the continuing existence of many debatable subjects which are not fundamental to the work of the gospel ministry. The Puritans used to say, 'The devil never lets the wind of error blow long in the same direction.' His purpose

[1] David Brown, *Life of John Duncan* (Edinburgh: Edmonston & Douglas, 1872), p. 474. For another writer in the same tradition, see *The Works of Andrew Fuller* (Edinburgh: The Banner of Truth Trust, 2007), pp. 370-1; 704-5.

[2] 'The mere controversialist, who would always be in the thick of the fight with error, is no more worthy of respect than the pugilist. The controversial minds are like the lean cattle of Egypt; they are very greedy, and are none the fatter for their feeding.' John Duncan, *Colloquia Peripatetica,* ed. William Knight (Edinburgh: Oliphant, Anderson,& Ferrier, 1907), p. 70.

is to keep side-tracking Christian leaders from their main work. Professor John Frame has listed twenty-one controversies which he believes have engaged evangelical Reformed Christians among themselves in the last seventy years.[1] Whatever one thinks of the issues Frame covers, it is surely a sad thing how much time was taken up in these disputes. Ministers of the gospel are called to awaken sinners and to lead them to Christ and glory. The time is short in which to do it. Our strength is small. Unless we are watchful, precious time will go to little purpose and opportunities for greater things be lost forever. Matthew Henry gave this wise counsel:

> Ministers should avoid, as much as may be, what will occasion disputes; and would do well to insist on the great and practical points of religion, about which there can be no disputes; for even disputes about great and necessary truths draw off the mind from the main design of Christianity, and eat out the vitals of religion.[2]

In eighteenth-century Scotland a Secession took place from the Established Church of Scotland that incorporated numbers of the best people and preachers in the land. The Secession was

---

[1] See his chapter, 'Machen's Warrior Children', in *Alister E. McGrath and Evangelical Theology,* ed. Sung Wook Chung (Grand Rapids: Baker, 2003).

[2] W. T. Summers, *The Quotable Matthew Henry* (Old Tappan, NJ: Fleming Revell, 1982), p. 71. Related to this subject is the question how far Christians should engage in apologetics. Spurgeon, when reviewing two orthodox authors who were defending the Scripture from the attacks of men claiming to speak on behalf of science, believed that their efforts were 'to little purpose. . . . Were you to take our advice, you would not argue. Love the gospel; live the gospel; practise the gospel; shame the adversaries. May be, God will give them repentance unto life.' He argues that to try to answer unbelievers on rationalistic grounds is to miss their real problem. (*The Sword and the Trowel,* 1883, p. 196.)

an evangelistic and missionary force for good. But the congregations which adhered to it were drawn into repeated controversies among themselves and with others. One of their most eminent ministers, John Brown of Haddington, left this testimony:

> I look upon the Secession as indeed the cause of God, but sadly mismanaged and dishonoured by myself and others. Alas! for that pride, passion, selfishness, and unconcern for the glory of Christ and spiritual edification of souls, which has so often prevailed. Alas! for our want of due meekness, gentleness. Alas! that we did not chiefly strive to pray better, preach better, and live better, than our neighbours.[1]

3. The danger of treating matters of belief as the only priority. Truth is indeed a priority. Error is to be resisted. False teachers are to be exposed. But it is not the only priority. If one asks the question, What should be the chief features of Christian behaviour according to the New Testament, it would be hard to argue that contending for the faith stands alone at the top of the list. Consider how much is said in Scripture on the believer as a peacemaker. 'Peacemakers', says our Lord, 'shall be called the children of God' (*Matt.* 5:9). 'If possible, so far as it depends on you, be at peace with all men' (*Rom.* 12:18). 'Pursue peace with all men' (*Heb.* 12:14). Within the church, the duty is 'being diligent to preserve the unity of the Spirit in the bond of peace' (*Eph.* 4:3). 'Have peace one with another', is the command of Christ (*Mark* 9:50); 'Be at peace among yourselves' (*1 Thess.* 5:13).

Or consider the biblical emphases on brotherly love. 'A new commandment I give unto you, that you love one another; as I

---

[1] *Life of John Brown, with Select Writings* (Edinburgh: The Banner of Truth Trust, 2004), pp. 70-71n.

have loved you, that you also love one another. By this shall all men know that you are my disciples, if you have love one to another' (*John* 13:34, 35). But what if a fellow-Christian sins against you? The answer is, 'forgiving one another, even as God for Christ's sake has forgiven you' (*Eph.* 4:32).

What such texts teach us is that the Christian life is more than a matter of knowledge and correct thinking. Spiritual life does not reside only in the intellect. A person can hold the right beliefs and not be a Christian at all. Where there is the new birth there is not only light to the mind, but love in the heart and grace in the spirit. Orthodox belief is not the only mark of true Christianity. When controversies begin between Christians they are tempted to forget this and attention may begin to turn solely on the points of difference. This was one of the problems of the church at Corinth. Knowledge was being treated as if it alone mattered. Some believed that they had got better knowledge and opinions than others, and there was something fundamental missing in their controversies. 'Knowledge makes arrogant'—'puffeth up'— 'but love edifies' (*1 Cor.* 8:1). 'Though I have all knowledge . . . and have not love, I am nothing' (*1 Cor.* 13:2). The truth defended without love is not genuine Christianity.

When disputes and differences arise they are not likely to be solved only by argument. Supernatural aid is needed. Thomas Manton wrote: 'In our contests about religion, God must especially be sought unto for a blessing . . . disputing times should also be praying times. Prejudices will never vanish till God "send out his light and truth", *Psa.* 43:3; and if the devil be not prayed down, as well as disputed down, little good cometh of our contests.'[1]

---

[1] Manton, *Works*, vol. 5, p. 264.

4. *The danger of underestimating how much combustible material there is still in the best of Christians.* Controversy can easily be the spark that ignites pride, conceit, ambition, and thus gives scope to the worst in human nature. It is sadly clear that some controversies in the churches show little concern for the glory of God.

Archibald Alexander wrote: 'It has long been remarked, that no spirit is more pungent and bitter than that of theologians in their contentions with one another; and it has often happened, that the less the difference, the more virulent the acrimony.'[1] How is such a thing possible if there are Christians on both sides? It is because in the heat of controversy the weakness and imperfection which beset us all are ignored. And we have an adversary who is well able to tempt us to wrong judgments and suspicions about other Christians. 'Satan knows that nothing is more fit to lay waste the kingdom of Christ than discord and disagreement among the faithful' (Calvin).

One temptation of the devil is to lead Christians to think that so long as they are defending the truth, and 'upholding the church', then other duties may be temporarily suspended. Who does not know that in controversy there are duties which almost pass out of sight? Christ's 'Golden Rule', 'Whatsoever you would that men should do to you, do you even so to them' (*Matt.* 7:12), is laid aside.[2] So is the royal law, 'You shall love your neighbour as yourself', and the apostolic command, 'Let each esteem other better than themselves' (*Phil.* 2:3).

---

[1] Quoted in James M. Garretson, *Princeton and Preaching* (Edinburgh: The Banner of Truth Trust, 2005), p. 135.

[2] Richard Baxter comments: 'In way of controversy we have many temptations to do as we would not be done by.'

When controversies start brotherly love can degenerate into meaning loving those who agree with me, or loving those who belong to the same party or denomination as I do. Robert Candlish has the evidence of church history supporting him when he writes of how brotherly love can turn into sectarianism and partisanship:

> You love as brethren those who happen to agree with you in holding certain opinions, pursuing certain ends. But if your unity is simply the result of your unanimity, it may make you strong as an ecclesiastical corporation; it may make you proud and happy as a select spiritual company, dwelling apart, nearer the throne than many. But it does not enlarge or elevate the heart. It is of the earth. It breeds earthly passions,—censoriousness, superciliousness, the bigot's mean intolerance. Such brotherly love has been the bane and curse of the Church in all ages, the scandal of Christianity, the fruitful mother of strife among its professors.[1]

5. *The danger of not foreseeing what desolations controversy can cause in the churches.* The evidence of church history is that times of controversy between Christians have commonly been followed by times of much deadness and lack of evangelistic success. That is not surprising, for contentions between Christians and churches grieve the Holy Spirit and encourage unbelief in the world. Unbelievers commonly may not understand the points of difference in controversies, but they can understand a worldly spirit, and when they see that operating among Christians they judge there is nothing supernatural in the faith.

[1] R. Candlish, *'The Christian's Sacrifice and Service of Praise,' an Exposition of Romans 12* (Edinburgh: Adam and Black, 1867), pp. 132-3.

Charles J. Brown, Free Church of Scotland leader of the nineteenth century, says this on Paul entreating the Christians at Philippi to unity: 'He knew that contention at once eats into the vitals of the Church itself, and exposes it to the ridicule and scorn of the world, stops the progress of the Gospel in Christians themselves and paralyses all their efforts to make it known to others. Therefore is he so intensely desirous to crush this evil in the bud.'[1]

Henry Coray, a witness to the divisions among men of Reformed persuasion after the death of Machen in 1937, left this testimony in 1981:

> In retrospect, there is probably not a person living who passed through those tumultuous years who does not look back on the fragmentation with sorrow and regret. Unfortunately in controversy emotions too often color principles, feelings run high, statements are tossed off that should never be voiced, personality clashes with personality, and scars of battle will be carried to the cemetery.[2]

How often we miss the warning of Scripture: 'The beginning of strife is as when one letteth out water' (*Prov.* 17:14), on which Charles Bridges writes: 'One provoking word brings on another. Every retort widens the breach. Seldom, when we have heard the first word, do we hear the last. An inundation of evil is poured in, that lays desolate peace, comfort, and conscience. Does not grace teach us the Christian victory, to keep down the expression of resentment, and rather bear provocation, than to break the bond of unity?'

---

[1] Published sermon by Brown (1806–84) on 'The Evils and Remedy of Discord in Religious Communities', from Philippians 2:1-4.

[2] Coray, *J. Gresham Machen, A Silhouette*, pp. 121-2.

John Newton as an example

John Newton was a peace maker. He lived at a time when there were some sharp disputes between evangelical Christians, and he stressed the catholicity that should mark all who belong to Christ:

> I profess myself to be of no party, and to love all of every party who love the Lord in sincerity. If they preach the truth in love, live as they preach, and are wise and watchful to win souls, and to feed the flock, I care not much whether they are called, Presbyterians, Congregationalists, Churchmen, Kirkmen, or Methodists . . . In some of the great shops of London, there are several counters; and servants at each attend the customers. If these servants are faithful and have their master's interests at heart, they will not be jealous of each other, they will not affront the customers by saying 'Why do you not come to be served on my side of the shop?' If they are all well served and pleased, it signifies not to which counter they come. Now what are we but servants of one great master? What are our denominations and distinctions but as the several counters?[1]

Newton was not the kind of easy-going pacifist who did not believe in controversy at all. But he has a good deal to say to gospel ministers, and especially to young ministers, on being drawn into controversy. We find him, for example, in correspondence with John Ryland Jr, a young preacher who has recently escaped from hyper-Calvinism. He now believed, as Newton believed, that the gospel is to be offered to all people. But his father, a veteran preacher, still leant on the side of hyper-Calvinism and put his belief into print. The son writes to Newton and asks whether he should go into print with his views, contrary to those of his

[1] *Wise Counsel: John Newton's Letters to John Ryland Jr,* ed. Grant Gordon (Edinburgh: The Banner of Truth Trust, 2009), p. 371.

father. In reply Newton grants the father has some failings, and then comments: 'He has not left many equal to him, in some respects. I would no more write against such a man, though he is not my father, than I would use my right hand to wound my left.' Newton gently suggests that Ryland Jr was too ready to get into combat, and writes: 'It seems errors are breaking out in the several places you mention, and you are on the point of writing to suppress them. But if there was a fire in all these towns, must they be burned to ashes, unless you can go with your bucket of water to quench the flames?' He urges him to concentrate on preaching the truth and to take 'less pains to combat and confute error.'[1]

Elsewhere Newton writes of the need for an earnest defence of the faith, but while he underlines that such work is praiseworthy and honourable, he says it is also dangerous: 'We find but very few writers of controversy who have not been manifestly hurt by it. Either they grow in a sense of their own importance, or imbibe an angry contentious spirit. . . . What will it profit a man if he gains his cause, and silences his adversary, if at the same time he loses that humble, tender frame of spirit in which the Lord delights, and to which the promise of his presence is made!'[2] If a Christian is convinced of his duty to enter into dispute with men teaching errors, then, Newton says, first, commend your opponent by earnest prayer 'to the Lord's teaching and blessing'. Then consider whether the opponent is to be regarded as a believer. In that case the Lord loves him, is patient with him, and 'you must

---

[1] *Ibid.,* pp. 256-7.

[2] Letter 'On Controversy,' *Works of John Newton,* vol. 1 (Edinburgh: The Banner of Truth Trust, 1988), p. 273. The same letter is in *Letters of John Newton,* (Edinburgh: The Banner of Truth Trust, 2011), p. 111.

not despise him, or treat him harshly. . . . In a little while you will meet in heaven; he will then be dearer to you than the nearest friend you have upon earth is to you now. Anticipate that period in your thoughts; and though you may find it necessary to oppose his error, view him personally as a kindred soul, with whom you are to be happy in Christ forever.'

But supposing you think the opponent is unconverted (a conclusion not to be reached without good evidence), then, 'He is a more proper object for your compassion than your anger. If God in his sovereign pleasure, had so appointed, you might have been as he is now. You were both equally blind by nature. If you attend to this, you will not reproach or hate him, because the Lord has been pleased to open your eyes and not his. Of all people who engage in controversy, we, who are called Calvinists, are most expressly bound by our own principles to the exercise of gentleness and moderation. If, indeed, they who differ from us have a power of changing themselves, if they can open their own eyes, then we might with less inconsistency be offended at their obstinacy.'[1]

In addition to Newton's letters, we have valuable information from another source on how he sought to practise his principles. The Rev. Thomas Scott served a parish not far from Newton's at Olney. When they first met, Scott did not believe in the Trinity and treated evangelical beliefs as matters for amusement. 'Once', Scott writes, 'I had the curiosity to hear him [Newton] preach; and, not understanding his sermon, I made a very great jest of it.' Yet he was drawn to Newton, and when Newton gave him an evangelical book, he wrote to him in the hope of engaging him

[1] Newton, *Works*, vol. 1, pp. 269-70.

in 'a controversial discussion of our religious differences'. 'My arguments', he believed 'would prove irresistibly convincing'. Accordingly about nine or ten letters passed between the two men, but to Scott's annoyance Newton would not debate theological points with him; instead he wrote of such things as the nature of true faith and how it is to be sought and obtained. For an interval of sixteen months this correspondence was dropped, but Newton treated his proud critic as a friend, and at length, when personal discouragements drove Scott to Olney for help, that friendship became one of the means God used to make Thomas Scott a new man and a leading evangelical writer. The whole story is told by Scott in a piece of autobiography, *The Force of Truth, An Authentic Narrative*.[1]

Conclusions

1. Men need to know themselves. Some by temperament are inclined to be pacifists in all disputes, and to decline controversy even when it is necessary. In that way errors and evils are often allowed to take root in churches unopposed. But much damage is also done by those who are too ready to take up issues, and even to enjoy strife. Thomas Scott, after his conversion, reflected on this problem, when he wrote, 'Mr Newton is, I think, too much afraid of controversy; others are too fond of it.'[2] Certainly all preachers

---

[1] *The Force of Truth* (Edinburgh: The Banner of Truth Trust, 1984). Newton's eight letters to 'Rev. Mr. S ****' were printed in *Cardiphonia* (see *Works of Newton*, vol. 1, pp. 556-618), or for five of these letters, with a good account of what took place, Josiah Bull, *Letters of John Newton* (Edinburgh: The Banner of Truth Trust, 2007), pp. 240-71.

[2] John Scott, *Letters and Papers of Thomas Scott* (London: Seeley, 1824), p. 123; see also pp. 316-7.

should be very sparing in taking up current controversies in the pulpit; a diet of criticism regularly delivered will produce a censorious people.

2. It is essential that time and energy be given to the main things. As Baxter wrote: 'Unholiness is the great point of difference . . . our towns and countries have two sorts of people in them; some are converted and some unconverted; some holy and some unholy; some live for heaven and some are all for earth; some are ruled by the word of God and some by their own flesh and wills.'[1] 'It is the principles and fundamental truths that life and death doth most depend upon, in which the essentials of Christianity do consist . . . Get well to heaven, and help your people thither, and you shall know all these things in a moment.'[2]

3. In all controversy unnecessary adverse comment on persons is to be avoided, and likewise the use of pejorative names and titles. After his early ministry, Spurgeon stopped describing fellow evangelicals as 'Arminians', while he continued to indicate his disagreement with their thinking. The use of offensive labels is more calculated to alienate brethren than to help them.

4. Brotherly love and humility are the great antidotes to wrong controversies. It is for the exercise of these graces that Paul entreats the disagreeing Christians at Philippi (*Phil.* 2:1-4). On which verses Charles J. Brown observed:

> There would be very little fear indeed, of Christians differing from each other, in anything of material consequence,—anything which they would find it necessary to make a matter of controversy in

[1] Baxter, *Practical Works,* vol. 4 (London, 1847), p. 662.

[2] Quoted by N. H. Keeble, in *Richard Baxter, Puritan Man of Letters* (Oxford, 1982), pp. 25, 29.

the Church,—if only they were thoroughly joined together in love and mutual affection. No doubt even the most attached and endeared Christian friends might differ in minor shades of opinion. But they would infallibly come to an agreement in things important and vital, so as to be, to all practical purposes, 'perfectly joined together in the same mind and in the same judgment'. It will be found to be the failure of love that principally, and in the first instance, gives rise to all formal and avowed differences and oppositions of sentiment among Christians.[1]

5. *This subject enforces our need of repentance.* How great is the unrecognized damage done in this area! We may be looking for spiritual success and yet at the same time be grieving the Spirit of God in God-dishonouring controversies. We too often treat contention with brethren as though it were contention against the world, forgetting the words of Samuel Rutherford; 'Why should we strive? For we be Brethren, the sons of one father, the born citizens of one mother Jerusalem . . . We strive as we are carnal, we dispute as we are men, we war from our lusts, we dispute from diversity of star-light and day-light.'[2]

[1] In this valuable sermon, Charles Brown further noted: "'Only by pride cometh contention." The reason is clear. Pride consists in the cherishing an extravagant opinion of oneself, one's rights, opinions, talents, acquirements, whatever. Pride concentrates its whole desires and affections upon the one object of self-advancement and gratification. Pride would take all, and give nothing. The happiness of the proud lies in seeing others beneath them. Humility, on the other hand, carries the soul away from self. The more humility, the more room in the heart for others. Loosening the affections from self, humility sends them forth upon all around. Opening the mind first to the glorious God, it next opens it to his creatures, his children.'

[2] Quoted from *Divine Right of Presbyteries* by John MacPherson, *The Doctrine of the Church in Scottish Theology* (Edinburgh: MacNiven & Wallace, 1903), p. 67. I have written on the issue of unity between churches in *A Scottish Christian*

How much damaging, discouraging strife can be found alongside a profession of faith in Christian unity! We confuse man's wisdom with the wisdom which is 'first pure, then peaceable, gentle and easy to be entreated' (*James* 3:17). How many of our words will be found as 'wood, hay, stubble' when 'the fire shall try every man's work of what sort it is' (*1 Cor.* 3:12, 13)? Boldness in opposing serious error is a need of the hour, but prayer for peace makers has surely taken too low place in our priorities, and we suffer for it.

6. *Wrong words arise from wrong thinking.* Hence the concluding exhortation of the apostle to believers whose unity was in danger. After reminding them of how prayer is indispensable for the possession of the peace of God, he tells them what they are to do with their minds—some things are always to be thought about, to be pondered: 'Finally, brethren, whatever is true, whatever is honourable, whatever is right, whatever is pure, whatever is lovely, whatever is of good repute, if there is any excellence and if anything worthy of praise, dwell on these things . . . and the God of peace will be with you' (*Phil.* 4:8, 9).

'Finally, brethren . . . be of one mind, live in peace; and the God of love and peace shall be with you' (*2 Cor.* 13:11).

Heritage (Edinburgh: The Banner of Truth Trust, 2006), pp. 277-310.

5

REST IN GOD:
THE FOURTH COMMANDMENT *IS* FOR TODAY[1]

Then God blessed the seventh day and sanctified it, because in it
he rested from all his work which God had created and made.

Genesis 2:3

W hat is believed about God is the most important thing
in life. And it is because man's greatest need is for the
true knowledge of God that the Bible stands alone. It is the only
revelation of God in words that he has himself given. To open its
pages is to be surrounded by truth about his being and nature.
Here are statements on which faith may be surely grounded, and
among these statements the text above is one of the most fundamental. It introduces us to two words which run through Scripture, the words 'sanctify' and 'rest'.[2]

---

[1] First published as a booklet by the publishers in 2010 and still available in
that format: *Rest in God & A Calamity in Contemporary Christianity* (ISBN: 978
1 84871 081 8).

[2] I am not here concerned to defend the historicity of the Genesis account of
creation. According to Scripture, understanding creation begins with faith (*Heb.*
11:3), which faith is itself born of the same creating power that brings the believer
from death to life (2 *Cor.* 4:6). Christ attributes the words of Genesis 2 to the

Both of these words speak to us of God. The first, to 'sanctify' means to 'make holy', 'to separate', or to 'set apart'. God himself is holy; uniquely that is his title. What he sanctifies is something which belongs to him, and the verse therefore indicates that in a special way the seventh day belongs to him. 'God blessed the seventh day and sanctified it.'

The second word, also introduced immediately after the creation, is 'rest',—God 'rested'. In the original, he *sabbatised,* from which came the word 'sabbath' (or 'rest'). The statement may appear a contradiction. How can an omnipotent Creator of the universe be said to 'rest'? Elsewhere in Scripture it is expressly denied that the Everlasting God can be 'weary or tired' (*Isa.* 40:28), and Christ denied that God ceased to work on the seventh day (*John* 5:17).

The explanation lies in a right understanding of the word 'rest'. It does not mean inactivity. It has to do rather with God's reflection on his completed creation. Six times in Genesis 1:4-25, we are told that all God made was 'good', and that chapter concludes, 'And God saw all that he had made, and behold, it was very good' (1:31). All was 'good' because all fulfilled the purpose for which he had created, namely, the display of his own glory. 'The heavens are telling of the glory of God' (*Psa.* 19:1). The world is the temple of God, 'and in his temple everything says, "Glory"' (*Psa.* 29:9). The splendour of creation—from flowers and birds, to oceans and furthest galaxies—declares to man that God is great and wise and good. All things come from God, and he is to be adored for all.

Creator (*Matt.* 19:4-5). 'The one who believes in the Son of God has the witness [testimony] in himself' (*1 John* 5:10).

'God rested' means that as he surveyed his work he was satisfied. He took pleasure in it, and that because he delights in his own glory. In other words, God's rest is in himself.[1] Augustine saw the meaning long ago when he prayed:

'After all thy works of creation which were very good, thou didst rest on the seventh day, although thou hadst created them all in unbroken rest . . . thou art the Good, and needest no rest, and art always at rest, because thou thyself art thine own rest.'[2]

Is Genesis 2:3 for us?

But for what purpose is this statement about God sanctifying the seventh day and resting made known to us? That question takes us to the reason why many pass lightly over the words of Genesis 2:3. An answer commonly given is that while the words speak about God, they include no mandate or direction for man to follow, no model for human behaviour. Therefore, it is said, any idea that a seventh part of man's time belongs in a special way to God is not taught in Genesis 2:3; it belongs rather to a much later date in Scripture, to the time of Moses.

---

[1] On the words the Lord 'rested and was refreshed' (*Exod.* 31:17, AV), Geerhardus Vos noted: '"Rest" has in Scripture, in fact to the Semitic mind generally, a positive rather than a negative import. It stands for consummation of a work accomplished and the joy and satisfaction attendant upon this.' (*Biblical Theology*, Edinburgh: The Banner of Truth Trust, 1974), p. 140. 'He took great complacency in what he had done, as that which was suited to the end aimed at, namely, the expression of his greatness, goodness, and wisdom, unto his rational creatures.' Owen, 'Exercitations Concerning the Name, Original, Nature, Use, and Continuance of a Day of Sacred Rest', *Exposition of Hebrews*, vol. 2, p. 334.

[2] Augustine, *Confessions and Enchiridion*, Library of Christian Classics, ed. Albert C. Outler (London: SCM, 1955), p. 332.

A great deal depends on whether this understanding of the verse is right or wrong. I offer these reasons for believing it is wrong:

1. The words 'God blessed the seventh day' are not the first notice of blessing in this narrative. There was blessing on the creation (*Gen.* 1:22), and blessing on man—'male and female he created them. And God blessed them; and God said to them, "Be fruitful and multiply, and fill the earth, and subdue it"' (*Gen.* 1:27-8). That God blessed a day for his own, and not for man's good, would be a usage of the word out of harmony not only with this passage but with the whole of Scripture.

2. It was clearly revealed to man at the beginning why he was created: 'God created man in his own image, in the image of God he created him; male and female he created them' (*Gen.* 1:27). Man was not made for himself. He exists for God and for fellowship with him. He was therefore made in the likeness of God. He is to love and delight in what God delights, that is, in God himself. That is the purpose of his existence (*Matt.* 22:37). It is unthinkable that this was true at the creation, and yet not known to man himself. To be holy as God is holy (*Lev.* 20:26; *1 Pet.* 1:16) was a truth implanted in man's very being, and therein lay his obligation to obedience. It is surely in the context of man's recognition of himself, as made in the image of God, with his life to be patterned on that of his Creator, that the words of Genesis 2:3 are to be understood. There is a day sanctified by God for man: as God rests in himself so man is to rest in God. *Therein lie true happiness and satisfaction.* By so marking the day, man was to enter into its blessing; glorifying God and enjoying God belong together. To quote Augustine again: 'Thou

hast made us for thyself, and our hearts are restless until they find their rest in thee.'[1]

If this is the right understanding of Genesis 2:3—and it is difficult to know any other—then we may conclude that the example of God stated in that verse was provided for man's imitation and instruction.[2]

3. The division of time into a seven-day week is best understood as originating at the creation and in connection with Genesis 2:3. Those who believe that a day of rest did not come into being until the law was given through Moses at Sinai have no explanation how a seven-day time cycle came to predate that event. But they reply, if a 'rest day' (Sabbath) came down from creation there would be references to it before Sinai. It is true there is an absence of such references, yet that is not altogether surprising. Man, after the Fall, instead of finding satisfaction in

---

[1] For a fuller treatment of what this means, see John Piper, *The Pleasures of God: Meditations on God's Delight in Being God* (Sisters, OR: Multnomah, 2000).

[2] That God 'sanctified' one day in seven for unfallen man is enough for us to know, without asking why it could be so if all man's days were to be lived for the glory of God. But the question is also relevant for the Christian. Abraham Kuyper gives this line of answer: 'Six days we have to spend in the fulfilment of our earthly duties, and one of the seven we have to consecrate to the more special service of the Lord. Of course, we should serve the Lord all the seven days. The difference between the two can never be other than a partial one. During the six days appointed to labour, all that concerns our outward life is prominent. On the Lord's day, on the contrary, it is the special service of the Lord that should dominate us . . . during the weekdays it is to a great extent a mediate serving the Lord, during and in our work, and that on the day of rest there should be an almost exclusive serving of our God in the immediate form of adoration and of drinking out of the Fountain of Life.' 'The Lord's Day Observance', Address by Abraham Kuyper in *Sunday the World's Rest Day* (New York; NY Sabbath Committee, 1916), pp. 56-7. Apart from a few chapters this is a poor volume.

God, preferred the creature to the Creator. In the words of Jeremiah, 'They have forsaken me, the fountain of living waters' (*Jer.* 2:13). Even so, traces of the rest originally appointed by God were not wholly obliterated. The passage of time in terms of seven days is noted in Genesis 8:10, 12, and in the life of Jacob we find Laban referring to the duration of a week (*Gen.* 29:27-8).[1] But where did such a division of time come from? Man could not deduce a seven-day week either from a solar year or from a lunar month. The best explanation for the week goes back to Genesis 2.

There is, however, stronger evidence that some knowledge of what God had earlier appointed survived. In Exodus chapter 16 there is a narrative of experiences that would otherwise be incomprehensible. Between the time of creation and the exodus from Egypt, thousands of years had passed. How unworthy the children of Israel were of their deliverance from Egypt is demonstrated by their behaviour in the wilderness. They complained that instead of being blessed by God they were likely to die of hunger, and God answered their unbelief by the miracle of which we read in Exodus 16:4-5: 'Then the Lord said to Moses, "Behold, I will rain bread from heaven for you; and the people shall go out and gather a day's portion every day . . . And it will come about on the sixth day, when they prepare what they bring in, it will be twice as much as they gather daily."'

'The sixth day' points to an existing knowledge of time divided by weeks. Still more significant, the text just quoted gives no explanation why, on the sixth day, twice the amount of manna would be given from heaven. The people were told that if manna

---

[1] 'Week' is not a Hebrew term as such, but the Hebrew word speaks of a period of seven days.

was kept overnight on any of five days it would become foul. But on the sixth day, when twice the amount was given, half was to be deliberately kept for eating on the following day. Accordingly we read of the sixth day: 'So they put it aside until morning, as Moses had ordered, and it did not become foul, nor was there any worm in it. And Moses said, "Eat it today, for today is a sabbath to the Lord; today you will not find it in the field. Six days you shall gather it, but on the seventh day, the sabbath, there will be none."' (*Exod.* 16:24-26). Some, not believing the word of God, and wanting manna every day, ignored the command of God and went out to collect it: 'but they found none' (16:27).

God specifically stated the purpose of this miracle, 'that I may test them, whether they will walk in my law or not' (16:4, NKJV). How could this be a test unless direction regarding the seventh day had not been already given? Nothing in Exodus 16 suggests that the appointment of a special seventh day of rest was only now being introduced. Had the manna miracle of Exodus 16 *followed* the giving of the Ten Commandments in Exodus 20, we would have understood the fourth commandment as the foundation for the 'test'. But that was plainly a later event at Sinai. Further, when we come to the wording of that fourth commandment, its language confirms that the Sabbath was not new but already existing. The commandment does not begin, 'Know there is a Sabbath day', but '*Remember . . .*'; and what is to be remembered is specifically identified with Genesis 2:3:

> Remember the sabbath day, to keep it holy. Six days you shall labour and do all your work, but the seventh day is a sabbath of the Lord your God; in it you shall not do any work, you or your son or your daughter . . . For in six days the Lord made the heavens

and the earth, the sea and all that is in them, and rested on the seventh day; therefore the Lord blessed the sabbath day and made it holy (*Exod.* 20:8-11).

To meet the force of the last paragraph, another explanation of the words it contains from Genesis 2 has been offered. It is that the words of Genesis 2:3 do not assert the establishment of the seventh day pattern at the time of the creation, but Moses inserted them at that point in Genesis because of what God meant to appoint for Israel at this much later date. So the quotation from Genesis 2:3 (in *Exod.* 20:11) was to give authority to a commandment intended only for the Jews, not for mankind. This interpretation surely requires a contorted reading of Genesis 2:3. It is the same as saying that God did not 'bless' any day at that time; rather, he delayed the blessing until a few thousand years later.[1] In the comment of Charles Hodge: 'It is an unnatural interpretation which no one would adopt except to suit a purpose. The narrative [of Genesis] purports to be what God did at the time of creation.'[2] Patrick Fairbairn attributes the origin of this idea to the 'fond conceit of some Jewish Rabbins, who sought thereby to magnify their nation, and was adopted only by such Christian divines as had already made up their minds on the temporary obligation of the Sabbath.'[3]

---

[1] David Green, in an occasional paper, has commented: 'Sabbath is the final blessing of three in the creation narrative (*Gen.* 1:22, 28; 2:3). Has anyone asserted that either of the first two blessings was delayed in their effect until God gathered Israel into a nation at Sinai? Why then should the third blessing be understood as delayed?'

[2] Charles Hodge, *Systematic Theology,* vol. 3, pp. 325-6.

[3] Patrick Fairbairn, *The Typology of Scripture,* vol. 2 (Edinburgh, T.&T. Clark, 1864), p. 127. 'Not what these men say, but what they prove, is to be admitted', is John Owen's comment on the Jewish Rabbins, *Hebrews,* vol. 2, p. 291.

This is a discussion of no minor significance. As I have said, a great deal depends on which conclusion is right and which wrong. If the appointment of the day of rest comes from the time of creation, then the words of the Lord, 'The Sabbath was made for man' (*Mark* 2:27) refer to all mankind, and the fourth commandment has divine authority today. If the appointment belongs to the time of Israel, then it has no universal significance, and the fourth commandment is only for Jews.

The Sabbath and ceremonial law

It is agreed on all sides that a fuller teaching on the Sabbath was given at the time of Moses, and that the nation needed to be educated or re-educated in its significance at that later period: 'You made known to them your holy Sabbath' (*Neh.* 9:14, ESV). The Sabbath was also at this time related to God's redemptive purposes. It was now a memorial not only of creation but of the nation's deliverance from Egypt (*Deut.* 5:15). The special day became a covenant sign of God's saving work in their midst (*Exod.* 31:16; *Ezek.* 20:12), and special sanctions of law were introduced for its observance by the nation. For its desecration the death penalty was appointed (*Exod.* 31:14-15). Even the lighting of fires was forbidden (*Num.* 15:32-36).

From this arises the argument that, whatever the origin of the Sabbath, it was so bound up with the nation that its permanence and its laws had to end when the Jewish economy passed away. It is said to be clear from the New Testament that ceremonial law, and law that belonged to Israel as a theocracy, terminated with the new covenant.

This argument depends on the assumption that the fourth

commandment is so identified with Israel that it could no longer have any place when the Old Testament economy passed away. To the contrary it may be said:

1. If the case we have given from Genesis 2:3 is sound, then it is already clear that the fourth commandment does not belong exclusively to the Jews.

2. In the Old Testament the observation of the fourth commandment was not required for Jews only but also for the 'sojourner [alien] who stays with you' (*Exod.* 20:10; see *Neh.* 13:16-18).

3. If the keeping of the Sabbath was only of ceremonial and not permanent moral significance, why was it placed by the finger of God in the centre of the moral law? The law is presented in Scripture as a reflection of the unchanging character of God. It came directly from God: 'And God spoke all these words, saying, "I am the Lord thy God . . ."' (*Exod.* 20:1-2), and it was written on tables of stone. To live for his glory, not to hate, not to commit adultery, not to lie, not to covet the possessions of another—these are abiding moral laws—and yet in the midst of these laws stand the words, 'Remember the Sabbath day, to keep it holy.'

Further, if the fourth commandment were only of ceremonial or temporary significance why should disobedience to it be treated in Scripture as a grave, moral offence? Generally the death penalty was not required for infringement of ceremonial law, but it was for this. There is no offence against God more seriously condemned by the prophets. Something much more than the ceremonial was involved in the commandment:

> A Sabbath-breaker was among the most vile and abominable characters. The whole day was to be devoted to God and religion.

When they kept the day as holy, they prospered. Calamities and judgments were inflicted on them, when as a nation they neglected God's holy Sabbath. All the prophets who were raised up, one after another, called them to observe the Sabbath, warned against any contempt of it, and placed the sanctification of the Sabbath upon the footing of equality with the moral virtues.[1]

4. A cessation from activity, and the observance of external rites, was never the essence of the fourth commandment (the idea that it was being a constant error among the Jews). A pause from the ordinary labours of life was always secondary to the primary spiritual object of the seventh day. The psalm designated 'for the Sabbath day' (*Psa.* 92), shows that the right observance of the day entails reflecting on the lovingkindness, the faithfulness, the uprightness of God. It is for delight in God. 'If because of the sabbath, you turn your foot from doing your own pleasure on my holy day, and call the sabbath a delight, the holy day of the Lord honourable, and shall honour it, desisting from your own ways, from seeking your own pleasure, and speaking your own word, then you will take delight in the Lord' (*Isa.* 58:13-14). This is in harmony with Genesis 2:3 and rest in God.

5. If the fourth commandment is to be considered redundant, and no longer part of the moral law of God, why is it that the New Testament, in repeated references to man's continued obligation to the law, makes no exception? The moral law, like its author, is 'holy, and just and good' (*Rom.* 7:12, AV). It has authority over Gentile as well as Jew (*Rom.* 2:15). Children at Ephesus were to be taught the commandments (*Eph.* 6:2). Timothy is to remember

[1] Nathan Perkins, *Twenty-Four Discourses* (Hartford: Hudson & Goodwin, 1795), p. 318.

that 'the law is good' (*1 Tim.* 1:8). The Apostle John says, 'Sin is the transgression of the law' (*1 John* 3:4, AV). Nowhere is there a suggestion of any exception. On the contrary James, quoting the Ten Commandments, writes that he who 'stumbles in one point . . . has become guilty of all' (*James* 2:10). In other words, there is a unity to the moral law. Like a sheet of glass, if broken at one point, the whole is shattered.

Calvin's correction

The authority of Calvin has often been quoted to support the view that the substance of the fourth commandment cannot be separated from the ceremonial law and that its authority is therefore ended for Christians. It is true this was Calvin's belief. In his *Institutes* he rejects the teaching that while 'the ceremonial part of this commandment has been abrogated . . . the moral part remains—namely, the fixing of one day in seven.'[1] But what has not been sufficiently noticed is that this did not remain the reformer's teaching. The passages on the fourth commandment found in the final edition of the *Institutes* of 1559 were written some years before that date and never revised. When preaching on Genesis, in 1559, Calvin very clearly takes the position which he earlier rejected:

> Concerning the creation of God's works, it is said that 'God rested in order to consider his works'. How can that be? He did not need to, as we have stated, but he instructs us what we are to do, as if saying, 'Behold, I want a day set aside for contemplation of my works.' Therefore, we have a God who is resting to be a mirror

---

[1] *Institutes of the Christian Religion*, II:viii:34. McNeill helpfully indicated the dates when the various parts of the *Institutes* were composed but he failed to note the significance of the dates in connection with the fourth commandment.

and pattern so that we may conform ourselves to him . . .[1] Because we are so weak and fragile and fickle, God has given us a day to help us sustain ourselves for the remainder of the week . . . help will come to us from the day itself which is given to us, during which we abandon all occupations, all worldly cares and thoughts in order to give our minds to that holy meditation we mentioned . . . Now in the Law, God commanded the day of rest for another reason, and at this point we must carefully distinguish between the order God established in the creation of the world and this commandment which appears in the Law of Moses . . . to give another and differing view, namely that it is a shadow and figure of spiritual rest . . . But the fact remains that we have one definite day of the week which is to be completely spent in hearing God's word, in prayers, and petitions and meditating upon his works that we may rejoice in him.

There are two facets of observance. For the present, it will suffice us to know that God continued in the Law what he had begun at the creation of the world . . . So let us learn to sanctify the day of rest in order to bring ourselves into conformity with our God's example and preserve the order which he established to be inviolable till the end.[2]

Calvin's change of judgment had already taken place by the time his *Commentary on Genesis* was published in 1554.[3] In that volume, on God's blessing of the seventh day in Genesis 2:3, he said:

---

[1] *Sermons on Genesis,* Chapters 1-11, trans. Rob Roy McGregor (Edinburgh: The Banner of Truth Trust, 2009), p. 123.

[2] *Ibid.,* pp. 128-30.

[3] J. K. Carter, in an unpublished doctoral thesis which I have not seen, traces the change in Calvin's thought to the years 1550–59; 'Sunday Observance in Scotland 1560–1606' (Edinburgh, 1957).

That benediction is nothing else than a solemn consecration, by which God claims for himself the meditations and employments of men on the seventh day. This is, indeed, the proper business of the whole of life, in which men should daily exercise themselves, to consider the infinite goodness, justice, power, and wisdom of God, in this magnificent theatre of heaven and earth. But, lest men should prove less sedulously attentive to it than they ought, every seventh day has been especially selected for the purpose of supplying what was wanting in daily meditation . . . he dedicated every seventh day to rest, that his own example might be a perpetual rule.[1]

The New Testament and the commandment

We are not yet done with the case that the New Testament has terminated the fourth commandment. Two arguments are advanced to support that case.

1. The Apostle Paul, it is said, speaks against treating particular days as special. He remonstrates with professing Christians for observing 'days and months and seasons and years' (*Gal.* 4:10). Regard for particular days he identifies with 'one who is weak in faith' (*Rom.* 14:1). In Colossians 2:16-17, 'a festival or a new moon, or a Sabbath day' are referred to as 'a mere shadow of what is to come'. These texts, it is said, leave no room for our treating one day in seven as still blessed and sanctified by God.

---

[1] *Commentary on Genesis* (Calvin Trans. Soc.; repr. Edinburgh: The Banner of Truth Trust, 1965), pp. 105-6. That the Genesis 2:2-3 pattern remains for us to follow today is again asserted in the reformer's final commentary (1563), *Commentaries of the Four Last Books of Moses*, vol. 2 (Calvin Trans. Soc.), p. 437. There are variations of emphasis in Calvin's thought which cannot be explored here. See *Institutes of the Christian Religion*, II:viii:28-34. Also, Fairbairn, *Typology of Scripture*, pp. 140-42, 513-21.

In response, it may be said that there is no certainty at all that these references have to do with the keeping of the seventh day. In the ceremonial law there were other 'sabbath days', that is festivals, in addition to the weekly Sabbath.[1] But supposing the words are understood to teach a prohibition for the keeping special of any day, then a considerable inconsistency would be found in the New Testament and in Paul's practice. For, clearly, there was just such a day observed in apostolic practice. Consider the evidence:

• The raising of financial aid for the needy was integral to the life of the churches, and Paul tells the church at Corinth, that the putting aside of aid for others was to be a duty on 'the first day of every week'. But this statement is introduced by words which show the direction was not one for observation at Corinth alone: 'Now concerning the collection for the saints, as I directed the

---

[1] 'Nor must it be forgotten that the Sabbath was under the Old Testament an integral part of a cycle of feasts which is no longer in force now. The type embodied in it was deepened by the Sabbatical Year and the Year of Jubilee. On the Sabbath man and beast rested, in the Sabbatical Year the very soil rests ... From all this we have been released by the work of Christ, but not from the Sabbath as instituted at Creation.' Vos, *Biblical Theology*, pp. 142-3. 'The Colossian Christian who declined the ceremonial observance of the Sabbath in this respect was right. An altogether different question arises when the Christian is asked to "secularize" the weekly Rest which descends to us from the days of Paradise, and which is as vitally necessary as ever for man's physical and spiritual well-being.' H. C. G. Moule, *Colossians and Philemon* (Cambridge: University Press, 1893), p. 110. On the words of Romans 14:5 ('One man esteems one day above another'), John Murray writes that to treat this as a reference to the Lord's day and the weekly sabbath, 'brings us into conflict with principles that are embedded in the total witness of Scripture.' It supposes that 'the beneficent design contemplated in the original institution (*Mark* 2:28) has no application under the gospel, and the lordship Christ exercised over the Sabbath was for the purpose of abolishing it.' John Murray, *Epistle to the Romans*, vol. 2 (Grand Rapids: Eerdmans, 1965), p. 259.

churches of Galatia, so do you also. On the first day of every week let each one of you put aside and save . . .' (*1 Cor.* 16:1-2).

• Acts 20:7 says something more on the practice of Christians on the first day of the week. When taking ship towards Syria, Paul stopped at Troas and stayed, writes Luke, seven days; it would be natural to believe that the reason for his staying lies in the words that follow: 'And on the first day of the week, when we were gathered together to break bread, Paul began talking to them, intending to depart the next day, and he prolonged his message until midnight.' The 'first day' has all the appearance of a stated meeting of Christians.

• Another apostle, the beloved John, writing by the Holy Spirit's guidance, adds information which is very significant. In an almost incidental reference, he indicates that the first day of the week was honoured by Christians with the highest of titles. A new name had entered history. On Patmos he writes: 'I was in the Spirit on the Lord's day' (*Rev.* 1:10). How can we be sure that in these words John was speaking of the first day of the week? Because of the testimony that exists from the earliest years of the post-apostolic age. The day which the Roman world called 'Sunday' was known to Christians as 'the Lord's day'. Ignatius, a younger contemporary of John's, who died about the year A.D. 107, spoke of Christians as 'no longer observing Sabbaths, but fashioning our lives according to the Lord's day, on which our life arose through him.'[1] For Christians the special day had become the first

---

[1] Ignatius, *Magnesians,* 9. Irenaeus, Tertullian, Clement of Alexandria, Origen and Cyprian, all speak of the first day of the week as 'the Lord's day'. Tertullian said: 'We celebrate the day after Saturday in distinction from those who call this day their Sabbath . . . All anxiety to be abstained from, and business postponed on

day of the week. In the words of Philip Schaff, one of the most dependable of historians, 'The universal and uncontradicted Sunday observance in the second century can only be explained by the fact that it had its roots in apostolic practice.'[1]

J. C. Ryle comments: 'Why we are told so pointedly about the "first day of the week" and the "Lord's day", if the Apostles kept no one day more holy than another, is to my mind inexplicable.'[2]

But if we accept this information, what does it have to do with believing that the Lord's day has any connection with the fourth commandment? The key question is this: if there was a transference of spiritual significance from the seventh day to the first, who authorised the change? To think the New Testament provides no light on that question is surely a mistake. The special day appointed by God in the Old Testament was surrounded

---

the Lord's Day.' Eusebius wrote: 'All things that it was duty to do on the Sabbath, these have we transferred to the Lord's day, as more appropriately belonging to it, because it has a precedence and is first in rank, and more honourable than the Jewish Sabbath. For in that day, in making the world, God said, Let there be light, and there was light; and on the same day the Sun of righteousness arose upon our souls.' When the early Christians were asked, 'Have you kept the Lord's day?' (*Servasti Dominicum?*), they replied, 'I am a Christian, I cannot but keep it' (*Christianus sum, omittere non possum*). For a fuller record of early church evidence see, 'The Literature of the Sabbath Question', (*British and Foreign Evangelical Review,* vol. 15, pp. 570-96), and R. T. Beckwith and W. Stott, *The Christian Sunday: A Biblical and Historical Study* (Grand Rapids; Baker, 1980).

[1] Schaff, *History of the Christian Church: Apostolic Christianity,* vol. 2 (Edinburgh: Clark, 1893), pp. 479. He adds: 'Such observance is the more to be appreciated as it had no support in civil legislation before the age of Constantine, and must have been connected with many inconveniences, considering the lowly social condition of the majority of Christians and their dependence on their heathen masters and employers.'

[2] Ryle, *Knots Untied* (London: National Protestant Church Union, 1896), p. 366.

by his authority. It was found in the first table of the law. It was not open for any man-made additions or alterations. God called it 'my holy day'. He alone regulated its use, and guarded it by solemn sanctions. Therefore when Jesus said, 'the Son of Man is Lord even of the Sabbath', he was claiming the prerogative of deity (*Mark* 2:28). Later, after asserting his possession of 'all authority in heaven and on earth', the Lord placed an all-important limitation on the authority of the apostles and the church with the words, 'teaching them to observe all that I have commanded you' (*Matt.* 28:20).

In the light of such words it is unthinkable that men changed the seventh day to the first without the authority of the One to whom that day belongs. That Christ's authority was behind the transference is surely implicit in the language of the Apostle John. In speaking of 'the Lord's day' he uses the very same language as is used of 'the Lord's Supper' (*1 Cor.* 11:20). 'The Lord's Supper' means the supper that Christ appointed and over which he presides. The first day of the week would not have been described as 'the Lord's' if Jesus had not himself commanded it.

I conclude, then, that the warnings of Paul against the superstitious use of days, and against the retention of national and ceremonial restrictions belonging to the Sabbath in the Mosaic economy, in no way invalidate the principle of one day in seven kept specially for God, as taught in the fourth commandment, and beginning with the Genesis pattern.

2. A second and last argument remains. In brief it is that the Old Testament commandment on the seventh day foreshadowed the 'rest' that was to come in Christ; therefore, for believers who have 'entered into rest', the meaning is now fulfilled, and to go

back to the commandment would be to go back to 'law'. Some would add, 'you are not under law but under grace' (*Rom.* 6:14).[1]

There is an important element of truth here. When rest in God was lost by man at the Fall, the divine purpose for the restoration of that rest lay in the future work of Christ. No man would come to that rest except he first come to faith in the promised Saviour. The fourth chapter of the Epistle to the Hebrews speaks of three 'rests': the rest of creation, when God rested from his works; the rest typified by the entering of Canaan; and the rest now obtained by Christ 'for the people of God'. 'For the one [*i.e.* Christ] who has entered his rest has himself also rested from his works, as God did from his' (*Heb.* 4:10).[2] As creation first gave delight and rest to God, the finished work of Christ is a yet more glorious rest. In that work Christ is 'satisfied' (*Isa.* 53:11), and in his 'beloved Son' the Father is 'well-pleased' (*Matt.* 17:5). United to Christ and righteous in him, we are redeemed for the glory of God, and see that glory 'in the face of Christ' (*2 Cor.* 4:6). Here is something greater than

[1] This text is often misunderstood. To be 'under law' is descriptive of all men by nature, it is to be under wrath. But Christ's fulfilment of the demands and penalties of the law places all who belong to him in an entirely new position. Their obligation to law has been met in Christ, and having received new life in him, sin no longer has the mastery over them. This is what Paul means by 'not under law'. Yet there is no contradiction when, at the same time, he asserts that in the gospel message, 'we establish the law' (*Rom.* 3:31, AV), indeed, that is the very purpose of the gospel (*Rom.* 8:4).

[2] This understanding of 'one who has entered his rest' is considered by many commentators to be speaking of the action of the believer; but if that were the case 'as God did from his' ceases to be of parallel, for the believer ceases from *sinful* works. See Owen, *Hebrews,* vol. 4, pp. 332-4. Some hold that the fourth commandment included a type, intended to teach Israel to cease from their own sinful works. I know no evidence for this opinion, save that all law in its Mosaic form brought home man's bondage to sin (*Gal.* 3:19-24).

the first creation. In the church God says, 'This is my resting place forever; here I will dwell, for I have desired it' (*Psa.* 132:14).

All this is wonderfully true, but why should the fulfilment of redemption make impossible the observance of a special day? Is it not rather entirely in harmony with revelation to believe that the first day of the week—the day when the early Christians greeted one another with 'Christ is risen!'—takes and continues what is in the fourth commandment and Genesis 2:3? Could any day be more suitable for special commemoration? Redemption has been accomplished: 'The stone which the builders rejected has become the chief corner stone. This is the Lord's doing; it is marvellous in our eyes. This is the day which the Lord has made; let us rejoice and be glad in it' (*Psa.* 118:22-24; *Matt.* 21:42; *Acts* 4:11).

It is granted that a dispensation of law under Moses was in preparation for Christ. Granted, too, that the gospel is a presentation of grace; but to go back to the practice of the substance of the fourth commandment—indeed to any of the Ten Commandments—is not to go to law as a means of justification, no more than the original pattern of Genesis 2:3 was in order to justification. The great difference for the Christian now is not that the law is no rule for him; it is that he has received a power and motive to obey that he never had before.

The Christian loves the law of God—'joyfully concurs' with it (*Rom.* 7:22)—not in order to gain acceptance with God, but because his nature is being restored to likeness with God. This was the great Old Testament promise of the New Covenant: 'For this is the covenant that I will make with the house of Israel after those days, says the Lord: I will put my laws into their minds, and I will write them upon their hearts. And I will be their God, and they shall be my people' (*Heb.* 8:10).[1] Or, stated in the clear language of fulfilment: 'For what the law could not do, weak as it was through the flesh, God did: sending his own Son in the likeness of sinful flesh and as an offering for sin, he condemned sin in the flesh, in order that the requirement of the law might be fulfilled in us, who do not walk according to the flesh, but according to the Spirit' (*Rom.* 8:3-4).

Christians have been set free to obey the law as 'the law of liberty'. They can say with William Cowper,

> *To see the law by Christ fulfilled*
> *And hear His pardoning voice*
> *Changes the slave into a child*
> *And duty into choice.*[2]

Of the fourth commandment Christ's words are therefore true, 'Do not think that I came to abolish the Law or the Prophets; I did not come to abolish, but to fulfil' (*Matt.* 5:17). The Pharisees had made the Sabbath a day of religious drudgery, of narrow external duties, all supposedly meritorious. This was what Christ rejected, but as Ryle says, he 'no more abolishes the Sabbath, than a man destroys a house when he cleans the moss or weeds off the roof'.[3]

---

[1] 'The law sends us to the gospel for our justification; the gospel sends us to the law to frame our way of life . . . We cry down works in opposition to grace in justification, and we cry up obedience as the fruits of grace in sanctification.' Samuel Bolton, *The True Bounds of Christian Freedom* (Edinburgh: The Banner of Truth Trust, 2001), pp. 11, 68-9.

[2] From the hymn, 'No strength of nature can suffice'.

[3] Ryle, *Knots Untied,* p. 365. 'So little does Jesus imagine that the Ten Commandments were of local and temporary obligation that he treats them as the law of the universal and eternal kingdom which he came to establish.' B. B. Warfield, *Shorter Writings* (Nutley, NJ: Presbyterian and Reformed, 1970), vol. 1, p. 313.

It is a serious misunderstanding of the New Testament to regard a careful obedience to the law of God as 'legalism'. On the contrary, it is proof of a true relationship with the Saviour. 'The one who says, "I have come to know him", and does not keep his commandments, is a liar, and the truth is not in him' (*1 John* 2:4).

Why should insistence on Sabbath observance be pharisaical or legalistic? The question is: Is it a divine ordinance? If it is, then adherence to it is not legalistic any more than adherence to the other commandments of God. Are we to be charged with legalism because we are meticulously honest? If we are jealous not to deprive our neighbour of one penny which is his, and are therefore meticulous in the details of money transactions, are we necessarily legalistic? Our Christianity is not worth much if we can knowingly and deliberately deprive our neighbour of one penny that belongs to him and not to us. Are we to be charged with legalism if we are scrupulously chaste and condemn the very suggestion or gesture of lewdness? How distorted our conception of the Christian ethic and of the demands of holiness has become if we associate concern for details of integrity with pharisaism and legalism! 'He that is faithful in that which is least is faithful also in much: and he that is unjust in the least is unjust also in much' (*Luke* 16:10, AV).[1]

The witness of history

Christians do not appeal to post-biblical history and tradition as authoritative revelation of the will of God. Nonetheless, if the question is asked whether there is evidence from history that God has continued to give special blessing through one day in

[1] John Murray, *Collected Writings,* vol 1, (Edinburgh: The Banner of Truth Trust, 1976), pp. 214-5.

seven, I believe there is. Repeatedly in periods when the Holy Spirit has revived the church, and when the Scriptures have been addressed with new seriousness, the fourth commandment has been recovered and there has been new health in the churches. While there was Sunday observance of a kind when the Reformation of the sixteenth century began, it was only when the power of the gospel was known that the spiritual keeping of the day was restored. Martin Luther preached,

> The Sabbath day is undoubtedly rooted in nature; in our human nature and in the nature of the created universe . . . It is Jehovah who made the Sabbath; though for man, the Sabbath is not of man, but has come to man as a gift of God himself.[1]

In the Puritan period which followed the Reformation in England, the life and power of Christianity were closely identified with the conviction that a seventh day blessing continues in Christ's appointment of the first day. Thus Thomas Brooks can write:

> Remember this, that there are no Christians in all the world comparable to those, for the power of godliness and the heights of grace, holiness, and communion with God, who are most strict, serious, studious and conscientious in sanctifying of the Lord's day.[2]

Likewise John Owen in 1671:

> If I have ever seen anything in the ways and worship of God wherein

[1] *Lectures on Genesis, Luther's Works* (Saint Louis, Concordia, 1958), vol. 1, p. 80.

[2] *Works of Thomas Brooks,* vol. 6 (Edinburgh: The Banner of Truth Trust, 2001), pp. 305-6.

the power of religion or godliness hath been expressed . . . it hath been there and with them where and amongst whom the Lord's day hath been had in highest esteem.[1]

The history of evangelical awakenings shows that an outpouring of the Spirit has brought a new desire to keep the Lord's day holy. So it was in Wales, in the Highlands of Scotland, and in many of the mission fields of the world, in the eighteenth and nineteenth centuries. One period of awakening in Wales began as John Elias preached one Sunday at Rhuddlan. It was the normal day for fairs and markets, and the place was crowded with those who had no thought of the fourth commandment. Friends had warned Elias that there was danger in what he proposed to do, but he went ahead, and on the steps of the New Inn preached on the words of Exodus 34:21, 'You shall work six days, but on the seventh day you shall rest; even during ploughing time and harvest you shall rest.'[2] The authority of God was so upon the word preached that the use of the Lord's day in that area was changed for generations to come.

The honouring of the fourth commandment has brought blessings to nations. Dr J. H. Merle d'Aubigné, visiting Britain in 1845, included these words in his description of the country:

One of the features which most completely brings out the character of British Christianity, is the observance of the Lord's day, or the

---

[1] Owen, *Exposition of Hebrews,* vol. 2, pp. 428-9.

[2] This remarkable occasion and its results are fully described in Edward Morgan, *John Elias: Life, Letters and Essays* (Edinburgh: The Banner of Truth Trust, 1973), pp. 86-89. See also pp. 397-99. Modern translations correctly render 'earing' as 'ploughing'; not that the Authorised Version is wrong, for ploughing is the meaning of the Saxon word 'erian' as the AV translators knew.

Sabbath as they term it, I think, improperly . . . I do not hesitate to say, that this submission of a whole people to the law of God, is very impressive and is probably the most incontestable source of the many blessings that have been showered on the nation. Order and obedience, morality and power, are all in Britain connected with the observation of the Sunday.[1]

On the other side of the Atlantic, Philip Schaff wrote of the Sabbath:

The due observance of it, in which the churches of England, Scotland and America, to their incalculable advantage, excel the churches of the European continent, is a wholesome school of discipline, a means of grace for the people, a safeguard of public morality and religion, a bulwark against infidelity, and a source of immeasurable blessing to the church, the state, and family. Next to the church and the Bible, the Lord's Day is the chief pillar of Christian society.[2]

It is true where 'keeping Sunday' has not been accompanied by a right understanding of the meaning of the day, the observance has become a dead formality. But among those whose intention is the honouring of God in the keeping of the day, the

---

[1] J. H. Merle d'Aubigné, *Germany, England, and Scotland, or Recollections of a Swiss Minister* (London: Simpkin, Marshall, 1848), pp. 105, 108-9.

[2] Schaff, *Apostolic Christianity,* p. 479. For the same conviction in J. C. Ryle, see *Knots Untied,* pp. 371-2. This belief was not confined to evangelical Christians. Lord Macaulay, speaking on the 'Ten Hours Bill' in Parliament, said, 'We are not poorer but richer, because we have, through many ages, rested from our labour one day in seven.' Prime Minister W. E. Gladstone believed: 'The religious observance of Sunday is a main prop of the religious character of the country. From a moral, social, and physical point of view, the observance of Sunday is a duty of absolute consequence.'

liveliest and happiest form of Christianity has commonly been found. This was once so evident that Robert Murray M'Cheyne could ask the question: 'Did you ever meet with a lively believer in any country under heaven—one who loved Christ, and lived a holy life—who did not delight in keeping holy to God the entire Lord's day?'[1]

On this subject our Lord's words surely remain relevant: 'You will know them by their fruits' (*Matt.* 7:16).

Conclusions

1. To quote Schaff once more:

> In the gospel dispensation the Sabbath is not a degradation, but an elevation of the week to a higher plane, looking to the consecration of all time and work. It is not a legal ceremonial bondage, but rather a precious gift of grace, a privilege, a holy rest in God in the midst of the unrest of the world, a day of spiritual refreshing in communion with God and in the fellowship of the saints, a foretaste and pledge of the never-ending Sabbath in heaven.[2]

2. Understanding the observation of the first day of the week as the day of Christ's resurrection points to the evangelistic imperative. No one but a Christian can begin a right keeping of the Lord's day. A spiritual day requires a spiritual life. As John Newton once wrote, 'How dull the Sabbath day, without the

---

[1] *Memoir and Remains of R. M. M'Cheyne,* ed. A. Bonar (Edinburgh: The Banner of Truth Trust, 2009), p. 601. Many in Scotland said this before M'Cheyne. For instance, John Willison (1680–1750): 'Wherever religion flourishes in the power of it, there it is that most conscience is made in the observation of the Sabbath.' *Practical Works of John Willison* (Edinburgh: Blackie, 1844), p. 111.

[2] Schaff, *Apostolic Christianity,* p. 479.

Sabbath's Lord'. There can be no delight in Christ's day until his resurrection and redeeming love are known. Only in the rebirth of a sinner does a recovery of the rest in the God of paradise begin. For this person, as Philip Henry once said, the command is 'an easy, sweet command'.[1] Those who come to Jesus for 'rest' sing with Charles Wesley,

> *Jesus, Thou art all I want,*
> *More than all in Thee I find.*

It was no great sacrifice for Eric Liddell in 1924 to pass by the opportunity for a gold medal in the 100 metres in the Paris Olympics rather than to run on the Lord's day. He was already enjoying something far greater.

A true understanding of the Lord's day must lead to compassion for non-Christians and a deeper concern to make Christ known. Ignorance of the fourth commandment is often an obstacle to salvation. 'I had no Sundays', was the admission of a dying London taxi driver, unprepared to leave the world.

> If the creation of the material universe should be kept in perpetual remembrance, how much more the new creation secured by the resurrection of Jesus Christ from the dead. If men wish the knowledge of that event to die out, let them neglect to keep holy the first day of the week; if they desire that event to be everywhere known and remembered, let them consecrate that day to the worship of the risen Saviour. This is God's method for keeping the resurrection of Christ, on which our salvation depends, in perpetual remembrance.

[1] J. B. Williams, *The Lives of Philip and Matthew Henry* (Edinburgh: The Banner of Truth Trust, 1974), vol. 1, p. 373.

God has given the world the Church, the Bible, the ministry, the sacraments; these are not human devices. And can it be supposed that the Sabbath, without which all these divine institutions would be immeasurably inefficient, should be left to the will or wisdom of men? This is not to be supposed. That these divinely appointed means for the illumination and sanctification of men, are in great measure without effect, where the Sabbath is neglected or profaned, is a matter of experience.[1]

3. The inability of non-Christians to keep the Lord's day in no way lessens their responsibility to keep it. The obligation rests upon the eternal principles set out in the moral law. Fallen man can, of himself, keep none of the Ten Commandments truly, yet he is still held to account for the obedience which God requires. Man's hostility to the fourth commandment is part of the antagonism with which he reacts to God himself (*Rom.* 8:7). Teaching the law of God, as Christ taught it, is a vital part of the witness of the church, for 'by the law is the knowledge of sin' (*Rom.* 3:20; 7:7, AV), for without that knowledge there is no repentance, and without repentance no salvation. Antinomianism, which discounts the Ten Commandments, is therefore contrary to biblical evangelism.

4. The moral law of God exists for mankind. Accordingly the Protestant nations professing Christianity buttressed the observation of the first day of the week with civil penalties. It was understood that reverence for God was necessary for the well being of a people and that it included respect for the day God has appointed. People have now largely forgotten how far this principle was once

[36] George W. Bethune, *Guilt, Grace and Gratitude* (Edinburgh: The Banner of Truth Trust, 2001), vol 2, p. 487.

embedded in national life. In the nineteenth century Charles Hodge could write in the United States:

> Christianity forbids all unnecessary labour, or the transaction of worldly business, on the Lord's Day . . . All public offices are closed, and all official business is suspended. From Maine to Georgia, from ocean to ocean, one day in the week, by the law of God and by the law of the land, the people rest.[1]

It is the argument of atheists that the state should have nothing to do with personal behaviour. Marriage law (until recently upheld by 'Christian' countries) stands on the same basis in Genesis 2 as does the seven-day cycle. Both should be upheld by governments. That contempt for God and the Ten Commandments brings judgments on nations is a clear truth in Scripture. And the most common form of such judgment is the removal of spiritual blessings (2 *Chron.* 36:17-21; *Jer.* 17:27; *Lam.* 2:6; *Ezek.* 22:26-31). An observation that William Hewitson once made in Germany has universal application: 'Germany tells me, that if Scotland lose her Sabbaths, she will lose along with them her religion and her God.'[2]

Some believe that for Christians to bear witness to the fourth commandment in an unsympathetic world would be to impede evangelism. The reverse has tragically proved to be true. Bishop Ryle understood what would happen in England if Sunday became as any other day:

> Break down the fence which now surrounds Sunday, and our Sunday schools will soon come to an end. Let in the flood of worldliness and pleasure-seeking on the Lord's day, without check

---

[1] Charles Hodge, *Systematic Theology,* vol. 3, p. 344.

[2] John Baillie, *Memoir of W. H. Hewitson* (London: Nisbet, 1874), p. 72.

or hindrance, and our congregations will soon dwindle away. There is not too much religion in the land now. Destroy the sanctity of the Sabbath, and there will soon be far less . . . It would be a joy to the infidel; but it would be an insult and offence to God.[1]

It is true that civil law can only restrain public disregard for the Lord's day, but to argue against the limited use of law to no use at all has been proved folly.

5. As already said, there ought to be no problem for Christians about how to observe the Lord's day. They will seek to 'remember' it before it comes, so that nothing is postponed to that day that can be done before. They will remember it is still a 'day' God has set apart from the ordinary engagements of life, and not part of a day.[2] Apart from works of 'necessity and mercy' the desire will be to arrange the day so that there is a maximum of time free from distractions of the affairs of the week. The faithful support of public worship ought to be beyond question, along with private time for spiritual things, especially for reading, meditation, and prayer. Christ is risen and he gives the Holy Spirit to us, as well as to the Apostle John on Patmos.

---

[1] Ryle, *Knots Untied*, p. 361. Ryle knew very well that Sunday laws make no one Christian, but they did something to keep the day special and to encourage church going. Many were brought to hear the Bible, and public respect for God spread through national life to a degree scarcely conceivable today.

[2] Sir Walter Scott observed, 'Give to the world one half of Sunday and you will find that religion has no strong hold on the other.' 'Not a part, but the whole day is the Lord's; and it is as dangerous to halve it with God in point of time, as it was for Ananias and Sapphira to halve their dedicated goods, and bring in but a part.' See John Flavel, on the fourth commandment, *Works* (Edinburgh: The Banner of Truth Trust, 1997), vol. 6, p. 234. R. L. Dabney closed a last letter to his children before his death with the words, 'Remember the Sabbath day to keep it holy.' T. C. Johnson, *Life and Letters of Robert Lewis Dabney* (Edinburgh: The Banner of Truth Trust, 1977), p. 523.

But as Christians know, there are complications in the right keeping of the day. The first responsibility belongs to heads of households (*Exod.* 20:10), and where that is neglected, believers may find—as Christian slaves in the first century—that in such households time is not freely their own. And what do believing parents do with children and young people in their families who, as yet, have no heart for spiritual things? The answer has to be along the lines of making the day as bright and happy for them as possible, while not neglecting the obedience God requires. Many who became Christians in later years have looked back on their Sundays in a serious Christian home as a great and formulating privilege. By parental example, as well as word, they were taught,

> *A Sabbath well spent*
> *Brings a week of content*
> *   And strength for the toils of the morrow;*
> *But a Sabbath profaned,*
> *Whate'er may be gained*
> *   Is a certain forerunner of sorrow.*

For young and old, the rest on earth prepares for the rest in heaven.

> There cannot be a more lively resemblance on this side heaven than the sanctifying of the Sabbath in a heavenly manner.[1]

> There can be, after the gospel, no blessing so high as that of the Sabbath, no privilege so great as that which it affords, no dignity so noble as that to which it introduces us.[2]

---

[1] Brooks, *Works*, vol. 6, p. 112.
[2] B. B. Warfield, *Shorter Writings* (Nutley, NJ: Presbyterian and Reformed, 1970) vol. 1, p. 309.

INDEX OF PERSONS CITED

THE OLD
Evangelicalism

**OLD TRUTHS
FOR A NEW
AWAKENING**

Iain H. Murray

Also by Iain H. Murray

The Old Evangelicalism:
Old Truths for a New Awakening

ISBN: 978-0-85151-901-2
226pp., clothbound

'The chief dangers that confront the coming century will be religion without the Holy Ghost, Christianity without Christ, forgiveness without repentance, salvation without regeneration, politics without God and heaven without hell.'

—WILLIAM BOOTH

Sin, regeneration, justification by Christ's righteousness, the love of God as seen in the cross, assurance of salvation—these are the truths that once thrilled churches and changed nations. Yet, where evangelicalism continues to affirm these truths, without such results, it is often assumed that she must have needs that cannot be met without something new.

In this book Iain Murray challenges that mindset. While the Bible not history is the textbook in these pages, Murray draws on the best authors of the 'old evangelicalism' to confirm what a glorious message the gospel is.

'. . . this is a good book, and the truths it proclaims urgently needed for our day when Evangelicalism is in a state of theological free fall and utterly unsure of its identity.'

—*Scottish Bulletin of Evangelical Theology*